|汉英对照|

传统文化标

TRADIT

中国关键词

KEYWORDS TO UNDERSTAND CHINA

中国外文出版发行事业局(CICG)
当代中国与世界研究院(ACCWS)
中国翻译研究院(CATL)

朝華出版社
BLOSSOM PRESS

First Edition 2023

Compiled by
China International Communications Group
Academy of Contemporary China and World Studies
China Academy of Translation

Translated by
Guo Yiming, Li Huiru, Xu Ruyi and Yu Hong
English text edited by
Cai Lijian, David Ferguson (UK) and Zhu Yuan

Cover designed by
Du Shuai

ISBN 978-7-5054-5223-7

Published by
BLOSSOM PRESS
24 Baiwanzhuang Street, Beijing 100037, China

Distributed by
BLOSSOM PRESS
24 Baiwanzhuang Street, Beijing 100037, China
Tel: 86-10-68995532
Fax: 86-10-68995258
Website: www.zhcb.cipg.org.cn
E-mail: zhbq@cipg.org.com

Printed in the People's Republic of China

《中国关键词：传统文化标识篇》
图书编委会

Keywords to Understand China
Traditional Culture
Editorial Committee

前言

中华优秀传统文化源远流长、博大精深，积淀了中华民族最深沉的精神追求，代表着中华文明的智慧结晶，为中华民族生生不息、发展壮大提供丰厚滋养，为人类文明进步提供重要支撑。中华优秀传统文化因特色鲜明而远博四方，因革故鼎新而永葆活力，其独一无二的理念、智慧、气度、神韵，不仅增添了中国人民内心深处的自信和自豪，也对各国人民产生强大吸引力。

为讲好中华优秀传统文化故事，集中展示中华文明的精神标识和文化符号，增进外国受众对中华文化文明的了解，“中国关键词”多语对外传播平台组织策划了《中国关键词：传统文化标识篇》。本篇按照思想文化、传统制度、科学技术、文学艺术、日常生活、自然风光与物质文化遗产的编写逻辑，综合借鉴“中华思想文化术语传播工程”等有关成果，选取百余条关键词进行重点介绍和解读，向各国读者呈现丰富多彩、生动立体的中华文化形象，推动中华文化更好走向世界。本书为中外对照版，由于能力及时间所限，在遴选编写中文词条时，难免挂一漏万。为使译文更符合目标语读者的阅读习惯，我们对翻译表达进行了创新探索，旨在提升读者的阅读体验。

“中国关键词”是中国外文出版发行事业局、当代中国与世界研究院、中国翻译研究院共同打造的国际传播品牌，主要围绕习近平新时代中国特色社会主义思想，进行中文词条专题编写、解读和多语种编译，通过平面、网络、移动端等多媒体、多渠道、多形态持续对外发布，旨在以外国受众易于阅读和理解的方式，阐释中国思想，解读中国理念，传递中国方案，分享中国智慧。

讲故事需要关键词，讲好中国故事需要中国关键词。让我们用“中国关键词”点击中国、沟通世界，促进中外文明交流互鉴。

Preface

Traditional Chinese culture has a long and rich history stretching back to antiquity. What is best in traditional culture embodies the Chinese nation's relentless pursuit of intellectual and spiritual growth and stands as a testament to its collective wisdom. It has nourished our nation, enabling it to survive and thrive, and helped propel the advancement of human civilization. Distinctive and fascinating, the best we have inherited from our ancestors have been spread far and wide around the globe. It endures, constantly refreshed through innovative transformation, and continues to flourish and shine with its unique concepts, its sparks of wisdom, its inclusiveness, and its unfailing elegance. Our traditional treasures are our sources of confidence and pride. They also appeal to and inspire the rest of the world.

This book, *Keywords to Understand China: Traditional Culture*, launched by our multilingual global communication platform "China Keywords", intends to provide global audiences a glimpse into traditional Chinese culture, by acquainting them with some of its most iconic elements. The book covers a wide range of topics, including philosophy and culture, traditional institutions, science and technology, literature and art, everyday life, and natural and cultural heritage. About 100 keyword entries are included in the book in a bilingual format, compiled on the basis of what has been done in this area, especially the multi-institutional project to introduce "Key Concepts in Chinese Thought and Culture".

We regret any unwarranted omissions that may have occurred in our selection of entries due to the limited time allocated for this project and our limited knowledge on related topics. In translating the entries, we opt for a target-oriented approach with the aim of enhancing the reading experience of our readers.

"China Keywords" is an international communication program jointly operated by the China International Publishing Group, the Academy of Contemporary China and World Studies, and the China Academy of Translation. Guided by Xi Jinping Thought on Socialism with Chinese Characteristics for a New Era, the program periodically rolls out complete sets of key terms on select topics with explanations and multiple language translations. They are published in different formats to allow wider access. In addition to the traditional print version, they are accessible online and on social media platforms to help global audiences better understand China's unique perspectives as well as its unique approaches and solutions to issues at hand.

Keywords are key to storytelling. To understand China, it is important to understand key concepts about China. This program aims to help build a bridge of understanding between China and the rest of the world and promote exchanges between civilizations.

目录
Contents

“中国”二字最早见于周朝（前1046–前256）青铜器“何尊”
The Chinese characters “Zhong Guo” (meaning China) were first discovered on the bronze vessel “He Zun” of the Zhou Dynasty (1046-256 BC).

思想文化

Philosophy and Culture

思想文化是民族生存和发展的重要力量。先秦时代被认为是中国文化的“轴心时代”，涌现出灿若群星的诸子百家，对后世产生深远的影响。佛教传入中国后，经历漫长的中国化过程，最终成为中国传统文化的重要组成部分。儒释道三教并立以及三教合一，形成中国传统文化的基本格局。这些思想文化的精华，按照传统经史子集的图书分类，保留在一些大型典籍之中，成为全人类的宝贵财富。

Ideas and culture are key to a nation's survival and development. The pre-Qin period is considered a pivotal period in the development of Chinese culture, in which many different schools of thought emerged, exerting a far-reaching influence on later generations. Buddhism, over a long period of localization after its introduction to China, gradually evolved into an important component of traditional Chinese culture. The coexistence of Confucianism, Buddhism and Daoism, and their later integration, constituted the basic framework for traditional Chinese culture. The best of what came out of this interactive process, as recorded in traditionally defined classics and history books, is a treasure of mankind.

太极图

太极图是中国古代一种文化符号，包含表示一阴一阳的图形，蕴含阴阳相生、刚柔相济的古老哲理。中国古人认为，太极为宇宙本原，宇宙中一切现象都由阴阳两个基本方面构成，两者既相互平衡、相互对立，又相互包含、相互转化。宇宙万物就在这种阴阳辩证关系的推动下循环运转、生生不息。太极图就是关于这一宇宙观的基本图示。其轮廓为圆形，代表作为宇宙本原及整体的太极；S形曲线将太极图分为形似鱼的两部分，黑色部分代表阴，白色部分代表阳；阴鱼中又有白色圆点，代表阴中有阳，阳鱼中又有黑色圆点，代表阳中有阴；阴鱼与阳鱼头尾相连，代表阴阳的相互转化和宇宙的循环运转。

这一图示简约而形象地表达了中华文明所蕴含的宇宙观，体现了和谐、对称、均衡、稳定、循环的丰富内涵。太极图元素在其他国家也有很多应用，例如，出现在蒙古国、韩国的国旗上等。

Taijitu Symbol (Taiji's Yin and Yang Symbol)

The Taijitu Symbol was a cultural symbol in ancient China, composed of a sign for yin and another for yang, representing ancient philosophical ideas. According to an ancient Chinese belief, the Taiji is the origin of the universe, in which every phenomenon is composed of two elementary aspects — yin and yang. The two are opposite but counterbalanced, mutually-containing while interconvertible. Everything in the universe goes on and on in cycles under the dialectical forces of yin and yang. The Taijitu symbol illustrates this concept. The symbol is round, representing the origin and oneness of the universe; an S-shaped curve splits the symbol into two fish-like parts — the black "fish" stands for "yin", and the white one "yang"; inside the yin fish there is a white spot, meaning the yang exists in the yin, and within the yang fish there is a black spot, meaning the yin exists in the yang. The yin and yang fishes are connected end-to-end, representing the interconvertibility of yin and yang as well as the circulation of the universe.

Simple as it is, the symbol graphically expresses the rich meanings of harmony, symmetry, balance, stability, and circulation that inform an outlook on life and the universe – a defining feature of Chinese civilization. The symbol is also used in many other countries, for example, on the national flags of South Korea and Mongolia.

《周易》

《周易》是中国先秦时期的传统典籍，包括经和传两部分。其中，《易经》分为图像和文字两部分，图像部分是64卦和384爻，文字部分称为卦辞、爻辞，是对卦、爻的说明。后续有解释和阐发卦辞和爻辞的作品《易传》，包括7种文辞共10篇，统称“十翼”（“翼”为辅助之义）。

《周易》原本是周代人卜筮所用的书。《周易》认为，宇宙万物均由阴、阳两个基本方面构成，以阳爻（—）和阴爻（- -）两种基本符号表示，称为两仪。两仪生四象，四象生八卦，两仪分别重叠，形成四象，四象再加阴阳爻，即阳爻和阴爻经三次重叠形成八卦（见图），八卦代表着自然界的八种现象。八卦相互重叠形成六十四卦，可以囊括自然界和

Zhou Yi (Changes of Zhou)

Zhou Yi is one of the classics of pre-Qin China, composed of *Yi Jing* (*The Book of Changes*) and *Yi Zhuan* (the Commentary to the Book of Changes, also called the 'Ten Wings'). *Yi Jing* is composed of graphics and texts: The graphics contain 64 Gua (hexagrams) and 384 Yao (6 lines per hexagram), and the texts are called *Gua Ci* and *Yao Ci*, which are descriptions of hexagrams and lines respectively. *Yi Zhuan* is a collection of ten pieces, comprising seven explanations and commentaries of the *Gua* and *Yao*, and it was known as "Ten Wings" (Wing means assistance).

Zhou Yi was originally a divination manual in the Zhou Dynasty (c. 1046-256 B.C.). According to Zhou Yi, yin and yang are the basic aspects of everything in the universe. The solid line "—" stands for the yang, and the broken line "- -" stands for the yin, together they are called *Liang Yi* (the two modes). The two modes generate the four images, and the four images give birth to the eight trigrams. The overlapping of the two modes forms *Si Xiang* (the four images). Different combinations of the yang and/or yin lines (unbroken and broken lines) give rise to Ba Gua or the eight trigrams (Qian☰, Kun☷, Kan☵, Li☲, Zhen☳, Gen☶, Xun☴, Dui☱), which represent eight basic natural phenomena (*Qian* for sky or heaven, *Kun* for ground or earth, *Kan* for water, *Li* for fire, *Zhen* for thunder, *Gen* for mountain, *Xun* for wind, and *Dui* for lake or marsh). Different combinations of the eight trigrams form 64 hexagrams, which can encompass all phenomena and their

人类社会的一切现象及其变化。

《周易》反映了中国古人对宇宙的认识，即宇宙始终处于变化之中，变化是宇宙的本质，只有变化才是永恒的。《周易》实际上就是对变化的认识和把握，被认为蕴含了宇宙万事万物的奥秘，在中国古代被誉为“群经之首”“大道之源”。

《周易》是中国古代杰出的哲学巨著，是中国传统思想文化中自然哲学与人文实践的理论根源，是中华民族智慧和精神的结晶。《周易》经过后世学者的不断阐释，形成了蔚为大观的“易学”，对中国几千年来政治、经济、文化等都产生了极其深刻的影响，其中蕴含的自强不息、厚德载物等内容成为滋养当代中国精神的重要源泉。

changes in nature and human society.

Zhou Yi reflects the ancient Chinese understanding of the universe — the universe is in a constant state of change, and as are the essence of the universe, change alone is eternal. *Zhou Yi* stands for the perception and the utilization of such constant change. This recognition and understanding of changes, or rather an attempt at explaining the mysteries of everything in the universe, places *Zhou Yi* at the top of all ancient classics.

A philosophical masterpiece of ancient China, *Zhou Yi* provides a theoretical framework for all studies in natural philosophy and social practices, embodying the wisdom and spirit of the Chinese nation. Later scholars made multiple attempts to interpret *Zhou Yi*, giving rise to a wealth of studies on this book with a profound impact on various aspects of political, economic, and cultural life in ancient China. The philosophical thinking elucidated in this book and related interpretation attempts informs the wisdom and spirit of the Chinese nation. It encourages self-improvement and extols moral strength. These ideas continue to nourish the spirit of contemporary China

四书五经

四书五经是中国古代儒家典籍的统称，包含“四书”和“五经”两个经典系统，详细记载了中国古代早期思想文化发展史上政治、军事、外交、文化等各方面的史实资料以及孔子、孟子等思想家的哲学思想，成为儒家思想的重要载体。

“五经”原本为“六经”，是六种上古时代流传下来的典籍，孔子（约前551—前479）及弟子等曾对其进行修订整理，因此成为儒家典籍。后来因《乐》亡佚，成为“五经”，它们分别是：《诗经》，中国最早的诗歌总集；《尚书》，是上古时代历史文献的汇总；《礼记》，记载了古代的制度和礼仪规范；《易经》，阐释了古人通过占卜探究宇宙和人事的方法；《春秋》，通过评价春秋时期以鲁国为中心的历史展现出深邃的政治智慧。西汉时期，汉武帝将儒家思想定为官方统治思想，“五经”成为当时政府选拔人才、制定政策、教化人民的重要依据。

Si Shu Wu Jing (Four Books and Five Classics)

Si Shu Wu Jing or the Four Books and Five Classics is a collective term for ancient Chinese Confucian classics. Comprising the "Books" series and the "Classics" series, these works contain detailed historical documents covering politics, military affairs, diplomacy and culture as well as ideas of thinkers like Confucius and Mencius, thereby serving as an important guide to Confucian philosophy.

The classics series originally consisted of Six Classics passed down from ancient times. Confucius (c. 551-579 B.C.) and his disciples edited and compiled them. Later, one of the classics, *Yue* (*Records of Music*), was lost, so only five now remain. They are: *Shijing* (*Book of Songs*), the first anthology of Chinese poetry; *Shangshu* (*Classic of History*), a collection of documentary records of events in China's ancient history; *Liji* (*Book of Rites*), a record of social norms and rites in ancient times; *Yijing* (*Book of Changes*), an explanation of how the ancestors explored the universe and human world through divination; and *Chunqiu* (*the Spring and Autumn Annals*), a historical book that offers insightful political wisdom via the official chronicle of the State of Lu back in the Spring and Autumn Period (c. 770-476 B.C.). During the Western Han Dynasty, Emperor Wudi (156?-87 B.C.) designated Confucianism as the official guiding principles, so the Five Classics became an important basis for the government to recruit talent, formulate policies, and educate the people.

“四书”指《论语》《孟子》《大学》《中庸》四种儒家典籍。《论语》《孟子》主要记载孔子、孟子的言行思想。《大学》《中庸》原本是《礼记》中的两篇，被宋代思想家朱熹提出来，与《论语》《孟子》并称“四书”。朱熹博采众长，为《四书》作了集注，他认为“四书”是儒学之根基，“五经”之阶梯。

在古代，四书五经是封建统治者治理国家的重要依据，也是每个知识精英的必读书，因此对中国社会和文化的发展产生了深远影响。四书五经作为中国传统文化的重要组成部分，在世界思想史、文化史上具有极高地位，在当代仍然是了解中国传统思想文化的重要书目。

The Four Books refer to *The Analects*, *The Mencius*, *The Great Learning*, and *The Doctrine of the Mean*. *The Analects* and *The Mencius* mainly record ideas attributed to Confucius and Mencius and stories about them. *The Great Learning* and *The Doctrine of the Mean* were originally two chapters from *Liji* (*Book of Rites*), until Zhu Xi (1130-1200), an ancient Chinese thinker of the Song Dynasty (960-1279), extracted them and compiled them into the Four Books together with *The Analects* and *The Mencius*. Zhu Xi also compiled annotations and comments for the Four Books based on some excellent works of others. He saw the Four Books as the basics of Confucianism and could serve as the step ladder to study the Five Classics.

The Four Books and the Five Classics were essential readings for the intellectual elite, and the ideas promoted therein constituted the philosophy of government throughout China's ancient period, exerting a profound influence on the development of Chinese society and culture. As an essential component of traditional Chinese culture, this collection occupies an important place in world history and remains an important reference source for understanding traditional Chinese thought and culture.

孔子

孔子（约前551—前479），春秋末期著名思想家、教育家，儒家学派创始人和主要代表人物。孔子开创了私人讲学的风气，打破了贵族对知识的垄断。据称，孔子有3000多名弟子，其中贤能者有72人。他曾带领部分弟子周游列国14年，晚年亲自修订了“六经”。孔子去世后，他的弟子和再传弟子将孔子及其弟子的言行记录下来，整理编成《论语》一书。这是了解孔子生平和思想的主要文献。

孔子主张恢复周礼，创造性地提出了以“仁”和“礼”为核心的思想体系。“仁”指个体内在本有的道德意识，以家庭伦理中的“孝悌”为起点和基础；“礼”则指一种合理的社会秩序，是“仁”的外在表现。“仁”与“礼”是贯通家庭、社会和政治生活的基本原则。

Confucius

Confucius (c. 551-479 B.C.) was a Chinese philosopher and educator of the Spring and Autumn period, and the founder and main representative of the Confucian school of thought. Confucius started the tradition of private teaching, which broke the nobility's monopoly of knowledge. He reportedly had over 3,000 disciples, of whom 72 were outstanding. Confucius toured around the states with some of his disciples for 14 years, and in his later life, he revised the Six Classics (Shi, Shu, Li, Yue, Yi and Chunqiu). After his death, his disciples and the disciples of his disciples collected and compiled their ideas and activities, which gave birth to *The Analects*, a key work for understanding the life and teachings of Confucius.

Confucius advocated restoring the rites of the Zhou Dynasty (1046-256 B.C.). He also proposed a creative philosophical system with "benevolence" and "rites" at its core. "Benevolence" refers to an individual's inherent moral consciousness, with filial piety and brotherly respect as the starting point and foundation of family ethics; "rites" refer to a reasonable social order, which is the external manifestation of "benevolence". "Benevolence" and "rites" are basic principles that run through family, social, and political life.

◀孔子像
Portrait of Confucius

孔子的思想和他整理的典籍经过后世的不断研习和阐释，深刻影响了中华文明数千年的发展，并对东亚、东南亚乃至欧洲文明发展影响深远。孔子也因此成为对中华文明影响最大的历史人物，在古代被尊崇为“至圣先师”，成为代表中华文明的标志性人物。

Confucian thought and the classics he compiled have been constantly studied and interpreted by later generations. They have had a profound impact on the development of Chinese civilization for thousands of years, and have left an indelible footprint across East Asia and even in Europe. The most influential figure in the history of Chinese civilization, Confucius was revered in ancient times as the "Supreme Saint and First Teacher", and is seen in modern times as the icon of Chinese civilization.

孟子

孟子（约前372—前289），战国中期著名思想家、教育家，是继孔子之后儒家学派的代表人物，与孔子并称“孔孟”。孟子一生经历与孔子非常相似，游历诸国都未得重用。孟子重要言行被编纂整理为《孟子》一书，他个性鲜明，言辞雄辩，不惧王权，有浩然之气。

战国时期百家蜂拥而起，儒家面临着其他学派的挑战。孟子以维护孔子思想为己任，在与其他学派的辩论中继承并发展了孔子的思想：他将孔子的“仁”扩充为仁、义、礼、智四种品德，并提出性善论，认为每个人都天生具有仁义礼智的萌芽，为儒家的道德主张奠定人性论基础；他将孔子的“为政以德”顺应民心发展为包含思想、政治、经济一系列具体举措的“仁政”，最早提出“民贵君轻”思想，强调国

Mencius

Mencius (c. 372-289 B.C.) was a famous thinker and educator during the middle Warring States period (475-221 B.C.) and a representative figure of the Confucian school of thought after Confucius. He is often mentioned together with Confucius as "Confucius and Mencius". He shared many similarities with Confucius in life experiences, as both of them toured around the states without being appointed to significant posts. His important ideas and activities were compiled into *The Mencius*, a testament to his strong personality, eloquence, and fearless refusal to be in thrall to royal power.

During the Warring States period, various schools of thought emerged and challenged Confucianism, and Mencius took it upon himself to defend and develop Confucius' ideas through debates with scholars from other schools. He expanded Confucius' concept of benevolence to include righteousness, propriety, and wisdom. He also proposed the theory of innate goodness, suggesting that everyone had the potential for benevolence, righteousness, propriety, and wisdom, thus laying the foundation for the Confucian theory of human nature. He developed Confucius' idea of "virtuous governance" – which called for responsiveness to the people's aspirations – into that of "benevolent governance" to be incorporated into a range of specific initiatives of an ideological, political, and economic nature. He was also the first to argue for the need to place the interests of the people before those of the ruler, emphasizing that the state had the obligation to protect the interests of the

家要以维护人民的利益为根本目标；他提倡国家间和谐稳定的关系应该以道德原则为基础，反对以力量强弱为基础；他强调儒家所讲的仁爱面对不同对象时，要有次序和程度的差别。

北宋以后，孟子的地位不断上升，被尊崇为“亚圣”（仅次于“圣人”孔子），他的著作《孟子》对中国文化的发展产生了深远影响。

people. He suggested that harmonious and stable inter-state relations should be based on moral principles rather than on strength, and emphasized that the Confucian concept of benevolence operated on different levels when applied to different sections of society.

After the Northern Song Dynasty (960-1127), Mencius continued to rise in status, and was revered as the "Second Sage" (second only to Confucius). *The Mencius* also exerted a far-reaching influence on the development of Chinese culture.

老子

老子是春秋末期著名思想家、哲学家，道家创始人和主要代表人物，被尊为道祖，称“太上老君”。春秋末年战乱，老子辞官归隐，西出函谷关，著有《道德经》。《道德经》分《道经》《德经》两篇，共八十一章，围绕“道”“德”的哲学理念，论述治国、用兵、修身、养生的道理。

老子建立了以“道”为中心的学说，认为道是天地万物的根源，德是事物自身的本性，道为体、德为用。他还进一步提出“道法自然”“清静”“无为”“守柔”等重要思想，认为无论是个人还是国家，都应该尊道贵德、顺道而行，才能实现个人的健康长寿和国家的长治久安。老子思想的核心是朴素的辩证法，认为世界上的任何事物都是相比较而存在的，相互对立的两个方面实际上是相互包含、相互渗透的，即“你中有我，我中有你”，并非一成不变。他在政治上主

Laozi

Laozi is a famous thinker, philosopher, founder and key representative of Taoism in the late Spring and Autumn period (770-476 B.C.). Considered as the ancestor of Taoism, Laozi is also called the Supreme Venerable Lord (Tai Shang Lao Jun). At the end of the Spring and Autumn period, Laozi resigned from office amid warring times and retreated to seclusion. He went westwards through the Hangu Pass and wrote *Tao Te Ching*. *Tao Te Ching* consists of two components, the *Tao Ching* (the Sutra of Way) and the *Te Ching* (the Sutra of Virtue), with a total of 81 chapters. Revolving around the philosophical concepts of *Tao* and *Te*, it discusses the principles of governance, military employment, self-cultivation and health preservation.

Laozi established a theory centered on *Tao*, believing that *Tao* is the root of all things in the world, that *Te* (virtue) is the nature of things themselves, and that *Tao* is the body and *Te* is the function. He further put forward important ideas such as "*Tao* operates naturally", "Quietness", "Inaction" and "Softness". He held that both individuals and countries should respect morality and follow the path of nature to achieve personal health and longevity, and long-term stability for a country. The core of Laozi's thought is simple dialectics. He believes that everything in the world exists by comparison, and that the two opposite aspects actually contain and permeate each other, that is, "there is me in you, and there is you in me"- a status that constantly changes. In politics, he advocated a small

张小国寡民、无为而治，在处世上强调柔弱不争，在修身上讲求返璞归真。很多流传至今的观念，如上善若水、道法自然、无为而治、祸福相依等都是来自《道德经》。

老子思想深深影响了中国人的哲学观念和思维方式，并对中国政治、宗教等产生了深远影响。其著作《道德经》被译为几十种文字在世界范围内传播，已成为全人类的宝贵精神财富。

country with less population be governed by doing nothing. He stressed on maintaining a soft character for worldly relations and returning to nature for self-cultivation. Many of his ideas that have been passed down to the present, such as "the highest good is like water", "*Tao* operates naturally", "governance through inaction", and "the interdependence between haps and mishaps", all have origins in *Tao Te Ching*.

Laozi's thoughts largely shaped up Chinese philosophy and ways of thinking, and had a profound impact on Chinese politics and religion. His book *Tao Te Ching* has been translated into dozens of languages and spread around the world as a piece of precious spiritual wealth of all mankind.

庄子

庄子（约前369—前286），战国中期著名哲学家、文学家，道家学派代表人物，与老子并称“老庄”。庄子崇尚自由，曾担任管理漆树园的小吏，后来辞官过着隐居生活。庄子最早提出“内圣外王”思想，其代表作收录于《庄子》。

庄子把宇宙看成起源于“道”的一个有机整体。庄子认为，“道”的存在先于宇宙万物，又在万物之中无所不在，万物都是“道”的一部分。“道”是宇宙万物运动的法则，其驱使万物而不受万物驱使，自然也是一切人类行为、思想的真正主宰。人如果得“道”，便获得了无限和自由。庄子将这种境界称为“逍遥”，“逍遥”就是心灵不被功名利禄等外物所拖累的自由自在、无拘无束的状态。

庄子擅长用寓言故事表达哲学主张，用神话传说的人物甚至山木骷髅、走兽昆虫来演绎故事，表达自己的哲学，对中国哲学思想和文学艺术发展产生了深远影响。

Zhuangzi

Zhuangzi (c. 369-286 B.C.) was a famous philosopher and literary writer during the middle Warring States period (475-221 BC). A representative figure of the Taoist school of philosophy, he is often mentioned together with Laozi as "Lao-Zhuang". He began his career as a minor official managing a lacquer tree garden. Later, he resigned from his position to live a reclusive life. He was the first to propose the idea of the inner virtues in a ruler. His signature works were collected in *The Zhuangzi*.

Zhuangzi saw the universe as an organic whole that originated from the "Tao". The Tao exists before all things and is omnipresent in all things; everything is part of the Tao. The Tao drives everything but is not driven by anything, and it is in control of all human behavior and thought. If anybody reaches the level of the Tao, they have achieved infinity and complete freedom. Zhuangzi referred to this state as "xiaoyao" or freedom from all restraints – spiritual liberation that enables a person to transcend worldly concerns.

Zhuangzi was adept at expressing philosophical ideas through fables. He created fables with figures from myths and legends, or even mountains, plants, skeletons, animals and insects, to illustrate his philosophical ideas, which had a far-reaching effect on China's philosophy as well as the development of literature and art.

墨子

墨子（约前468—前376），先秦时期著名思想家、教育家，墨家学派创始人和主要代表人物。墨家是儒家学派的主要理论对手，以“兼爱”反对儒家的社会等级制度，代表社会底层民众思想，与儒家并称“显学”，有“非儒即墨”之称。墨子的思想学说收录于《墨子》。

墨子倡导的“兼爱”具有平等与博爱的意思，要求君臣、父子、兄弟都要在平等的基础上相互友爱，爱别人就像爱自己。墨子认为，社会上出现强凌弱、富侮贫、贵傲贱的现象正是天下人不能兼爱所致。因此，国与国之间也应当兼爱，要坚持“非攻”的外交原则，战争不是治病的良方，要以德义服天下，以兼爱来消弭祸乱。

Mozi

Mozi (c. 468-376 B.C.) was a renowned thinker and educator in the pre-Qin period. He was the founder and a major representative of the School of Mohism. A major rival of Confucianism, Mohism advocated "inclusive love" (jianai) as opposed to the Confucian emphasis on an hierarchical social order. It reflected more what the people at the bottom of society had in mind. It was regarded as one of the two major philosophical schools of the time alongside – and often as an alternative to – Confucianism. The teachings and theories of Mozi were collected in the book *Mozi*.

Mozi's concept of "inclusive love" emphasized equality and universality, requiring monarchs, ministers, fathers and sons, and brothers to love each other on an equal basis, and urging people to love others just as they love themselves. Mohists criticized social ills such as oppression of the weak by the strong, exploitation of the poor by the rich, and discrimination of the lowly by the noble, which they believed resulted from the failure to embrace inclusive love. They also promoted a "non-aggression" principle in inter-state relations, believing that war was not an effective way to resolve conflicts and that rulers should seek to rule through virtue and inclusive love, rather than through military power.

◀《墨子》中的小孔成像现象示意图
Illustration of the pinhole image formation in "Mozi"

墨子有强烈的社会实践精神，对中国传统生产、科技、数学、物理、逻辑学等都有巨大的贡献。墨子首先定义了力，认为物体运动是因为有力的作用；发现了光沿直线传播；定义了“圆”“方”等数学概念；提出了系统的形式逻辑理论，成为中国古代逻辑思想体系的一位重要开拓者。

Mozi was also keen on solving practical problems and contributed significantly to the development of China's traditional economy, technology, mathematics, physics, and logic, among others. He was the first to define force in mechanics, and believed that the movement of objects was caused by the application of force. He discovered that light traveled in straight lines; defined mathematical concepts of circle and square; and proposed systematic theories of formal logic, making him a pioneer in developing ancient China's system of logic.

韩非

韩非（约前280—前233），战国末期著名思想家、哲学家，法家学派代表人物。他融合并发展了“势”“术”“法”，并发展形成完备的理论体系，为封建社会的君主制度提供依据。后人将其思想整理编纂成《韩非子》。

韩非是一位现实主义思想家，认为人性好利是一切行为的基本逻辑，政治的起源正是社会利益冲突的产物，矛盾和斗争才是政治生活的常态。韩非认为，国家要实现持久稳定的发展不应当寄希望于贤能的统治者，而应当着力于制度建设。处上位的统治者要学会采取以静制动、以虚控实的方法，配合“因任授官”“信赏必罚”的组织管理“技术”，实现对官僚队伍的管理。

韩非推崇依法治国，强调统治者依法执政、官员依法行政、民众依法行事，才能维持中央集权国家的持久稳定。自秦以后的大一统王朝中，韩非的理论得到了充分的应用和发展，对后世产生很大影响。

Han Fei

Han Fei (c. 280-233 B.C.) was a famous thinker and philosopher of the late Warring States period (475-221 B.C.). A representative scholar of the Legalist school of thought, he integrated and developed the concepts of "Shi" (power or authority), "Shu" (methods or techniques), and "Fa" (laws) to create a complete set of theories to justify the feudal monarchical system. Han Fei's ideas and theories were collected in *The Hanfeizi*.

Han Fei was a realist who believed that human nature was driven by self-interest, that politics originated from conflicts of interests in society, and that contradictions and struggles were the norm of political life. He believed that a state could not rely on wise and capable rulers to ensure sustained prosperity, but should focus on institutional development. He advised rulers to learn how to rely on peace to control movement and rely on transcendence to control reality. At the same time, he emphasized the need for a bureaucratic structure that ensured the appointment of officials on the basis of ability and accountability that rewarded good performance and punished bad behaviors.

Han Fei promoted the idea of ruling the state by law. He emphasized that only when the ruler governed according to the law, bureaucrats followed the law, and the populace abided by the law, could a centralized state maintain lasting stability. Han Fei's theories were applied and developed during the periods that witnessed high levels of centralization after the Qin Dynasty (221-206 B.C.), exerting great influence on later generations.

《孙子兵法》

中国古典军事著作《孙子兵法》相传为春秋时期军事家孙武（前545—约前470）所著，是中国现存最早的兵书，也是世界上最早的军事著作，被誉为“兵家经典”“百代谈兵家之祖”。

《孙子兵法》分为十三篇，高度概括了中国古代的战争经验和战争理论，详细论述了战前准备、策略运用、作战部署、敌情研判、为将之道和用兵之法，不仅探讨了政治、经济、外交等与战争的关系，而且讨论了天文、地理、气象等诸多因素对于战争的影响，对中国古代军事思想和战争实践具有重要指导意义。该书高度理性地审视战争，主张“不战”“慎战”，以最小代价获取最大胜利，认为战争的最高境界不是通过战争打败敌人，而是以谋略战胜敌人，斗智不斗力。

《孙子兵法》内容丰富、思想深邃、逻辑缜密、行文灵活，是中国古代军事思想精华的集中体现，对军事、经济、政治等领域产生重要影响，在世界军事史上也具有重

The Art of War of Sun Tzu

The Chinese classical military work *The Art of War of Sun Tzu* is said to have been written by Sun Wu, a military strategist in the Spring and Autumn period (770-476 B.C.). It is the earliest existing military book in China and also the earliest military book in the world. The book is known as the "classic of military strategists" and Sun Wu "the ancestor of a hundred generations of military strategists ".

In 13 chapters, *The Art of War of Sun Tzu* effectively generalizes the war experience and war theory in ancient China, and discusses in detail pre-war preparations, strategy application, combat deployment, enemy situation research and judgment, commanding as a general and mobilization of troops. It not only discusses the relationship between politics, economy, diplomacy and war, but also discusses the influence of many factors such as astronomy, geography, and meteorology on war. It is of significant guiding value for ancient Chinese military thought and war practice. The book examines wars in a highly rational way, advocating "no war" and "exercise of caution before entering into a war" so as to obtain the greatest victory at the least cost. Sun Wu believed that the highest level of war is not to defeat the enemy through war, but by strategy, and fight wits, not force.

The Art of War of Sun Tzu is rich in content, profound in thought, rigorous in logic, and flexible in writing. This encompassing compilation of the essence of ancient Chinese military thought has a profound impact on military, economic, political

要地位。《孙子兵法》被翻译为多种语言畅销海外，不少国家还将其列为军校教材和管理指南，用于指导军事战略和商业管理。

and other fields, cementing itself an important position in the world military history. *The Art of War of Sun Tzu* has been translated into many languages and sold well overseas. Many countries have chosen it as a textbook and management guide for the spheres of business and military.

朱熹

朱熹（1130—1200），南宋时期著名的思想家、理学家，被后人尊称为“朱子”。理学是宋代儒者吸收佛教、道家思想而形成的一整套思想理论体系，是中国古代哲学的高峰。理学的核心问题是处理天理与人欲、理与气、性与情、道与心等之间的关系。

朱熹是宋代理学的集大成者，他系统总结了北宋理学的成果，建立了庞大而成熟的心性论、理气论、宇宙论、历史哲学与朱子理学。朱熹的理学思想强调天理是支配宇宙万物的根本法则与规律，人修养的最大目标就是使“心”与“理”合一。

朱熹的思想学说（“朱子学”）于13世纪初就开始传入朝鲜、日本及越南等国，对东亚儒学的发展产生了深远影响。

Zhu Xi

Zhu Xi (1130-1200) was a famous thinker and Confucian philosopher of the Southern Song Dynasty (1127-1279). He was revered as Master Zhu by later generations. Developed on the basis of assimilating Buddhism and Daoism, neo-Confucianism represents a new high water mark for ancient China's philosophical research. The core issue of Neo-Confucianism is the relationship between the principles of heaven and human desires, principles and vital force, nature and emotions, and the Tao and the mind.

Zhu Xi put together Neo-Confucian theories developed in the Song Dynasty, systematically building on the achievements of other Neo-Confucianists to develop a huge and mature set of philosophical concepts, covering the study of the mind, the theory of principles and vital force, cosmology, historical philosophy, and the Zhu Xi school of thought. Zhu Xi's Neo-Confucianism emphasizes that the principles of heaven are the fundamental law that governs all things in the universe, and that the ultimate goal of self-cultivation is to align the mind with the principles of heaven.

Zhu Xi's philosophy began to spread to neighboring countries such as Korea, Japan, and Vietnam in the 13th century and shaped the development of Confucianism in East Asia.

王阳明

王阳明（1472—1529），明代著名哲学家、教育家、军事家。王阳明通过对儒家思想的审视，反对盲目服从封建伦理道德，而是强调个人能动性，提出“心即理”的重要学说、“致良知”的哲学命题和“知行合一”的方法论，被后世称为“阳明心学”。

王阳明力倡心学，提出“天下无心外之理，无心外之物”，而“良知”是心的本体，是人先天具有的道德善性和认知本能，一切德性皆出于此。他强调，要去除“物欲”的遮蔽，从自己内心去寻找“理”，充分彰显心中固有的“良知”，将良知、天理推及到事事物物中去，即“致良知”。在知与行的关系上，王阳明提倡“知行合一”，反对将知行分作两截，认为知中有行，行中有知，二者不能分离，也没有先后。

王阳明的思想学说在明代之后流传甚广，流派众多，还传播到了日本、朝鲜等东亚国家，对当地思想文化和社会

Wang Yangming

Wang Yangming (1472-1529), a famous philosopher, educator and strategist in the Ming Dynasty (1368-1644). Having carefully reviewed Confucianism, Wang Yangming opposed blind obedience to feudal ethics and morality, but emphasized individual initiative, put forward the important theory of "mind is reason", the philosophical proposition of "conscience" and the methodology of "unity of knowledge and action", collectively called "Yangming's Mind Theories" by later generations.

Wang Yangming strongly advocates the theories of mind, and proposed that "there is neither reason nor a thing outside a person's mind", while "conscience" is the noumenon of the mind, the innate moral goodness and cognitive instinct of human beings, from which all virtues come. He stressed that we should remove the cover of "material desire", find "reason" from within, fully demonstrate the inherent "conscience" in our hearts, and extend conscience and heavenly principles to everything, that is, "to reach conscience". In terms of the relationship between knowledge and action, Wang Yangming advocates the unity of the two, and opposes separating knowledge from action. He believes that there is action in knowledge, and there is knowledge in action. The two cannot be separated and neither is more superior than the other.

Wang Yangming's ideology and theory spread widely after the Ming Dynasty, offshoot into many schools, and spread to Japan, Korea and other East Asian countries, leaving a deep mark on the local ideology, culture and social developments

发展产生重要影响。王阳明是中国古代思想家中哲学思想的集大成者，他重视人的德性修养和主观能动性，提出“心即理”“致良知”“知行合一”等思想理念实现了理论与实践的统一、主观与客观的统一、内圣与外王的统一，在当今时代亦具有重大的理论价值和现实意义。

there. Wang Yangming is the epitome of philosophy among ancient Chinese thinkers. He paid attention to the cultivation of human virtue and subjective initiative, and puts forward "mind is reason", "reaching conscience", "unity of knowledge and action", fermenting the unities of theory and practice, of subjective and objective, of internal saints and external kings, bearing great theoretical value and practical significance even till today.

道教

中国本土宗教道教，以“道”为最高信仰，是在中国原始宗教、民间信仰、神仙方术等的基础上，以黄帝之学和老子之学为理论依托而建立起来的宗教。道教以黄帝为始祖，以老子为道祖，以张道陵为教主，以《道德经》为根本经典。

东汉时期，张道陵（34—156）首创五斗米道，将老子及《道德经》加以宗教化，实现道教的组织化、仪式化。隋唐五代和北宋时期，道教思想逐渐体系化，以道为核心的社会观、自然观和神仙观等教义和教观渐趋完整。道教认为，人的生死祸福、寿命长短，取决于人自身。人通过积德行善、不断修炼，可以达到与道合一的境界，从而能够长生久视、得道成仙。因此，道教创造了很多修道养生的方法，如炼丹、辟谷、服食、导引、静坐等。

道教对中国古代政治、经济、科学技术、文化艺术、民风民俗等方面都产生了深远的影响。道教文化是中国古代文化遗产的一部分，在中国传统文化中有重要地位。

Taoism

Taoism, a Chinese native religion, takes "Tao" as the highest belief. It is a religion established on the basis of Chinese primitive religion, folk beliefs, immortal alchemy and the theories cultivated by Yellow Emperor and Laozi. Taoism takes the Yellow Emperor as its ancestor of origin, Laozi ancestor of doctrine and Zhang Daoling celestial ancestor, and *Tao Te Ching* as the fundamental classic.

During the Eastern Han Dynasty (25-220), Zhang Daoling (34-156) pioneered the Way of the Five Pecks of Rice (Wu Dou Mi Taoism), and canonized Laozi and *Tao Te Ching*, ritualized Taoism with proper organization. During the Sui (581-618), Tang (618-907), Five Dynasties period (907-960) and the Northern Song Dynasty (960-1127), Taoism thought became systematic, and the social view, natural view and immortal view with Taoism as the core gradually took shape. Taoism believes that life and death, happiness and misfortune, and longevity depends on the person himself. Through accumulating virtue, doing good deeds, and practicing Taoism, people can achieve the state of unity with the Tao, live a long life and become immortals. Therefore, Taoism has created many ways to practice the doctrine and maintain health, such as alchemy, fasting, food-taking, guidance, meditation, etc.

Taoism has had a profound impact on ancient Chinese politics, economy, science and technology, culture and art, folk customs and other aspects. Taoism is an integral part of Chinese ancient cultural heritage and plays an important role in traditional Chinese culture.

《金刚经》

《金刚经》全称《金刚般若波罗蜜经》，是大乘佛教的重要经典之一。《金刚经》有七种汉文译本，以西域僧人、翻译家鸠摩罗什（344—约411）的译本最为流行，在中国流通广泛，注疏众多，影响至今。这部经书篇幅不长、文字通俗、思想深刻，阐述了早期大乘佛教提倡的般若学说。“般若”是梵语“Prajñā”的音译，意为智慧，专指如实认识一切事物和万物本源从而解脱成佛的特殊慧识。《金刚经》就是阐述这种般若智慧的佛教典籍。唐朝咸通九年（868）的《金刚经》木刻本，是目前世界上有年代可考、刻印精细、保存完好的早期的雕版印刷精品。

《金刚经》作为大乘佛教的核心典籍，对中国佛教各宗派都有深远的影响。六祖慧能（638—713）一系的禅宗南宗更是以《金刚经》立宗，在中国佛教大为兴盛，并流行至

Jin Gang Jing (*The Diamond Sutra*)

The "*Jin Gang Jing*" or the "Diamond Sutra", also known as "*Jingang Bo're Boluomi Jing*" (Sanskrit: Vajracchedikā Prajñāpāramitā Sūtra), is an important classic of Mahayana Buddhism. The *Diamond Sutra* has seven Chinese translations, but the most popular and widespread of these was translated by Kumārajīva, a monk and translator from the ancient Kingdom of Kucha (in what is now Xinjiang, China). Many annotations and commentaries were written based on this version, which is still influential nowadays. The "*Jin Gang Jing*" is not a lengthy work, but it interpreted the profound "*Bo're*" concept in the early stage of Mahayana Buddhism in plain language. "*Bo're*" is the Chinese transliteration (Mandarin pinyin) of the Sanskrit "*Prajñā*," meaning wisdom, and in Mahayana Buddhism it refers to the special wisdom of knowing the truth of all things and their sources in the original way, through which one can free oneself and achieve Buddhahood. The "*Jin Gang Jing*" is a Buddhist classic that carries this wisdom. The woodblock-printed version of the *Jin Gang Jing* in the ninth year of the Xiantong reign of the Tang Dynasty (868) is the earliest traceable copy, delicately carved, printed, and well-preserved.

As a core classic of Mahayana Buddhism, the "*Jin Gang Jing*" has had a profound influence on all the sects of Chinese Buddhism. Hui Neng, the Sixth Patriarch of *Chan* Buddhism, founded the Southern *Chan* school of Buddhism based on the "*Jin Gang Jing*", which has remained popular in China even to this day. In turn, under the influence of the "*Jin Gang Jing*",

今。深受《金刚经》影响的中国化佛教，对唐宋之后的思想文化尤其是对宋明理学影响巨大。以“禅”为特质的艺术形式，如禅诗、禅画、禅乐等逐渐得到古代官员和知识分子的认可，由此深刻影响了中国人的艺术审美和文学创作。

Buddhism with Chinese features played an essential role in the emergence of Neo-Confucianism in the Song Dynasty (960-1279) and the Ming Dynasty (1368-1644). Art forms inspired by Chinese *Chan* Buddhism, such as *Chan* poetry, Chan paintings and Chan music won gradual acceptance from ancient officials and scholars, and helped shape aesthetic tastes and inform literary creation.

六祖慧能

六祖慧能（638—713），亦称惠能，是佛教禅宗南宗创始人，也是中国佛教禅宗六祖，倡导“直指人心，见性成佛”的顿悟。以慧能为代表的禅宗，流传时间最长，是中国本土文化特色明显的中国佛教宗派。

慧能认为，人人皆有佛性，人人皆可成佛，佛和众生之间，差别在于是迷还是悟，迷悟只在一念之差。只要消除妄念，回归自性，一念之间就可以觉悟成佛。他还主张，修行离不开生活，行住坐卧皆是禅，这为中国禅宗的世俗化、生活化奠定了理论基础。慧能创立的佛教禅宗给中国古代哲学思想和宗教文化的发展带来重要影响，对古代中国和世界的审美、诗歌、绘画、文学也都影响深远。慧能弟子根据慧能的事迹和言论整理成《六祖坛经》，它是中国僧人撰述里唯

Sixth Patriarch Hui Neng

Hui Neng (638—713), the sixth patriarch of China's Chan Buddhism, was the founder of the Southern Chan School of Buddhism. He promoted the idea of "sudden enlightenment/awakening" through which one could "discover Buddhahood that is already in his nature". Hui Neng's Chan Buddhism is the sect that sustained for the longest time in China and was infused with rich Chinese cultural symbols.

According to Hui Neng, the Buddha's nature is within every common person and everyone can achieve Buddhahood. What distinguishes the Buddha from common people is enlightenment, although enlightenment is just one step away from ignorance. Enlightenment and Buddhahood can be achieved in a flash of thought when one eradicates unfounded ideas and returns to one's nature. Hui Neng also advocated that Sādhanā or spiritual cultivation cannot be separated from life: People's everyday activities — walking, standing, sitting or lying — are all ways of practicing Chan. His ideas laid a theoretical foundation for the secularization and popularization of Chinese Chan Buddhism.

Chan Buddhism significantly influenced the philosophical thoughts and religious culture in ancient China, while exerting far-reaching impacts on aesthetics, poetry, painting and literature in both ancient China and the wider world. The disciples of Hui Neng compiled *Liu Zu Tan Jing* or the *Platform Sutra of the Sixth Patriarch*, based on Hui Neng's life events and teachings. *Liu Zu Tan Jing* is the only work with the title of

一被称为“经”的著作，也是研究中国和世界佛教史、哲学史、文化史的重要典籍。

Jing among all monk-related works in China; it serves as an important reference for studying Chinese and global his-tory of Buddhism, philosophy and culture.

三教合一

三教合一，就是中国儒家、佛教与道教思想，保留各自特点，相互会通、合流的现象，形成了以儒家为主，佛教与道教为辅的基本格局，融合发展成为中华文化的主流，对中国思想史、文化史产生持久且深刻的影响。

佛教自从传入中国后，就一直与儒家、道教互相借鉴与融合。魏晋南北朝时期是三教融合的第一次高潮，佛教思想吸收儒家忠孝的伦理，逐渐本土化、中国化；而道教吸收儒家伦理、道家哲学与民间信仰，借鉴佛教的僧团寺庙组织与仪式，其理论、组织架构、仪式等逐渐成熟。隋唐时期，三者进一步融合。佛教主动吸收儒家的中庸思想与道家的自然思想，最终形成具有中国特色的佛教宗派禅宗、净土宗与律宗。北宋时期，三教融合又一次达到高潮，儒家吸收佛学、道家思想，形成“理学”，道教吸收儒家、佛教思想，其修

Integration of Three Religions

The integration of three religions refers to the fusion of Confucianism, Buddhism and Daoism even though each preserves its respective features. A basic framework thus emerged with Confucianism at its core, complemented by Buddhism and Daoism, and became a dominant force in Chinese society, exerting a profound and far-reaching influence on China's history of thought and culture.

After Buddhism was introduced to China, a process of mutual learning among Buddhism, Confucianism, and Daoism and their integration began to unfold. During the Wei (220-265), Jin (265-439), and the Southern and Northern Dynasties (420-581), this integration reached a peak. Buddhism absorbed the Confucian ethics of loyalty and filial piety, gradually finding its way into local life and increasingly exhibiting Chinese cultural features. Daoism incorporated Confucian ethics and folk beliefs, while drawing on the experience in how Buddhist temples were organized and rituals performed, a move that allowed Daoism to develop a mature set of theoretical principles of its own, a more sophisticated organizational structure and more established rituals. The Sui (581-608) and Tang (608-907) dynasties witnessed further integration of the three schools of thought. Buddhism began actively absorbing the Confucian concept of the Golden Mean and the Daoist idea of staying true to one's nature, leading to the emergence of Chan Buddhism, Jingtu (Pure Land) Buddhism, and Lüzong (Vinaya) Buddhism – sects with Chinese characteristics. In the Northern

养理论与方法更加内化。元明清时期，三教融合进一步发展。明代哲学家王阳明以儒家为主，融合佛教、道教思想，提出“心学”。同时，道教、佛教在晚明时期表现出世俗化、入世化的趋势。

“三教合一”反映了中国本土文化与外来文化之间的“交融性”，深刻体现了中华民族包容、和平、开放的精神气质与文明品格，这也是中华文明历久弥新的重要原因。

Song Dynasty, the integration of the three schools reached yet another climax. Neo-Confucianism came into being by absorbing Buddhist and Taoist ideas. Taoism went on to absorb more Confucian and Buddhist thoughts and internalized the concept of self-cultivation and the way it was practiced. This integration of the three schools continued throughout the Yuan (1206-1368), Ming (1368-1644) and Qing (1616-1911) dynasties. The Ming Dynasty philosopher Wang Yangming developed the study of the mind by incorporating ideas from Buddhism and Taoism into Confucianism. Meanwhile, in the late Ming Dynasty Taoism and Buddhism increasingly found their way into secular life.

The process of the integration of the three religious traditions showcased how China's homegrown culture converged with imported cultural elements, reflecting the inclusiveness and openness and a longing for peace of the Chinese nation. These qualities also explain the resilience of Chinese culture over time.

《史记》

《史记》是西汉著名史学家司马迁（约前87年—?）撰写的一部纪传体史书，记载了上至上古传说的黄帝时代，下至汉武帝太初四年（前101年）间共3000多年历史，被列为“二十四史”之首。《史记》以历史上的帝王等政治中心人物为史书编撰的主线，包括十二本纪（历代帝王政绩）、三十世家（诸侯国和汉代诸侯、勋贵兴亡）、七十列传（重要人物的言行事迹）、十表（大事年表）、八书（各种典章制度），共130篇，52万余字。

《史记》是中国最早的通史，其首创的纪传体编史方法为后来历代“正史”所传承，对后世史学发展产生深远影响。《史记》在中国文学史上具有重要地位，书中生动展现了历史人物命运起伏，世事变迁，其作者司马迁更被后世尊称为“史迁”“史圣”。《史记》提出著书目的是研究自然规

Historical Records

The *Historical Records* is a biographical historical book written by Sima Qian (about 87 B.C. -?), a famous historian in the Western Han Dynasty (206 B.C.-A.D 25). It records the legendary era of the Yellow Emperor from the ancient times to the fourth year (101 B.C.) of Emperor Wudi of the Han Dynasty (206 B.C-A.D 220), covering a history of more than 3000 years, hence considered as the primary piece among *Twenty-four Histories*. The *Historical Records* focuses on emperors and other political central figures in history, containing 12 Benji (the achievements of emperors in previous dynasties), 30 aristocratic families (the rise and fall of the vassals, princes and the nobility in the Han Dynasty), 70 biographies (the words and deeds of important figures), ten chronicles (the chronology of events), and eight books (various rules and regulations), with a total of 130 articles and more than 520,000 words.

The *Historical Records* is the earliest general history of China. Its method of compiling history in the form of biography has been inherited by the "official history" of later dynasties and generates a long-lasting impact on the development of later historiography. The *Historical Records* is also well-known in the history of Chinese literature. It vividly shows the ups and downs of the fate of historical figures and the vicissitudes of the world. Its author Sima Qian is honored as "Shi Qian"(History Qian) and "Shi Sheng" (History Sage) by later generations. The viewpoint that the purpose of this book is to scrutinize relationship between the laws of nature and human

律与人的关系、古今社会变化规律，成一家之说的观点，对中国历史学影响深远，书中许多人物积极进取等精神品质，深刻影响了中国人的价值取向和精神气质。

beings, the laws of social changes in ancient and modern times and, hopefully establish a school, has an intense impact on Chinese historiography. The proactive and enterprising spirits displayed by many figures in the book were examples for the larger Chinese population and affected the values and characters of such to a great extent.

《资治通鉴》

《资治通鉴》是由北宋司马光（1019—1086）主编的一部编年体史书，主要以时间为纲、事件为目，从公元前5世纪末到10世纪中期，涵盖十六朝1362年的历史，史料价值极高，在中国古代史书中占有极重要的地位。司马光和《史记》作者司马迁被后人并称“史学两司马”。

《资治通鉴》分三部分，将年表、帝纪、历法、天象、目录、举要及索引集于一块，开创了编年体史书多功能目录的新体例，内容包括政治、军事、民族关系、文化、经济和历史人物评价等，总结了16个朝代国家盛衰、民族兴亡的经验教训，为当朝君主治国理政提供借鉴。《资治通鉴》是历代帝王将相、文人骚客、各界要人必读著作，也是一部深入理解中国传统政治运行的经典著作。

Zizhi Tongjian

Zizhi Tongjian (*Historical Events Retold as a Mirror for Governance*) is a chronology of history mainly compiled by Sima Guang (1019-1086) in the Northern Song Dynasty. It covers over 1362 years of Chinese history spanning 16 dynasties from 403 B.C.-A.D. 959. An invaluable reference book of history, it is of great importance among Chinese historical records. Sima Guang is revered as one of the two great "Sima historians" in Chinese history, the other Sima being Sima Qian, who wrote *Records of the Grand Historian*.

Zizhi Tongjian integrates in three parts annals, imperial records, calendars, celestial signs, contents, abstracts, and indexes, creating a new style of multi-functional cataloging for works of history. It covers politics, military affairs, ethnic relations, culture, the economy, and comments on historical figures, and summarizes the lessons and experience of 16 dynasties and their rise and fall, serving as a reference book on governance for monarchs. *Zizhi Tongjian* was a must-read for emperors, officials, and scholars. It offers a deep insight into how the traditional political system functioned in China.

《永乐大典》

《永乐大典》是中国古代史上规模最大的类书，编撰于明代永乐年间。这部集中国古代典籍于大成的分类资料工具书，保存了中国自先秦时期到明代初期的典籍资料多达七八千种，收录了文学、哲学、历史、天文、地理、宗教、技术、艺术等各类内容，全书共22877卷，11095册，约3.7亿字，堪称中国古代最大的百科全书。该书编纂队伍达到2196人，1407年定稿，朱棣亲自作序并赐名《永乐大典》。全书于1408年才抄写完毕。

《永乐大典》巧妙地采用“用韵以统字，用字以系事”的编排方式，依据音韵分出单字，从大量典籍中汇集和该字有关的词条，再整段、整篇、整部地抄录与该词条有关的文献内容，并注明出处，配有图画，由此清晰、详细、全面地保留了大量古籍，涵盖了中华民族数千年来的知识财富。遗憾的是，《永乐大典》正本下落不明，副本屡遭火灾、战乱或失窃，现存世界各地的版本不到原书的4%，但依然为后

Yongle Encyclopedia

Compiled during the reign of Yongle Emperor of the Ming Dynasty (1368-1644), the *Yongle Encyclopedia* was ancient China's largest collection of classic works with entries listed by categories. As a massive reference tool, it featured over 7,000 kinds of works from the pre-Qin period to the early years of the Ming Dynasty, covering a wide range of topics including literature, philosophy, history, astronomy, geography, religion, technology, and art. The collection comprised 22,877 chapters (rolls) in 11,095 volumes, totaling about 370 million Chinese characters. A total of 2,196 people were involved in compiling the collection, and when it was finished in 1407, Zhu Di, Emperor Yongle himself wrote the preface for it and named it the *Yongle Encyclopedia*. Not until 1408 was the final copy completed.

The encyclopedia's compilation was unique in its clever use of rhymes to display Chinese characters to guide the reader to related subjects. For the purpose of indexing, Chinese characters were arranged according to their rhymes, which led to entries from numerous classics, replete with paragraphs, passages or even whole books related to those entries. At the same time, all the sources were noted, and corresponding illustrations included. This well-categorized, comprehensive collection reflected thousands of years of Chinese intellectual wealth. Unfortunately, however, the original copy of the encyclopedia was lost, and the duplicates suffered from fire, war, or theft, and now no more than 4% of the original texts

世提供了珍贵资料。中国国家图书馆是世界上《永乐大典》馆藏最多的地方，现存224册，只字片纸都弥足珍贵，蕴藏着中国的精神之源。

have survived. Notwithstanding, it has still proved to be of great value for later generations. Currently, the National Library of China holds most of what has remained of the Yongle Encyclopedia — a total of 224 volumes, a treasure trove of evidence pointing to China's cultural glory.

《四库全书》

《四库全书》是清代编修的一部大型丛书，由清乾隆皇帝（1711—1799）亲自主持，纪昀等著名学者、官员360余人负责编撰，近4200人抄写，前后历时15年（1773—1787）完成。全书收录了先秦时期至清代乾隆以前2000多年间的重要典籍3500余种，共计79300余卷、36000余册，约8亿字，是中国古代规模最大的丛书。

全书按照中国古代图书分类法分为经、史、子、集四部，故称“四库”。经部收录儒家经典及相关著作，史部收录历史类书籍，子部收录诸子百家相关学术著作，集部收录诗文词总集和专集等。全书封面按照春、夏、秋、冬四季的顺序标明书的类别，分绿、红、蓝、灰褐四色装潢书册封面，以便于检阅。为便于保存和传播典籍，全书编成后又誊抄7

Siku Quanshu

The *Siku Quanshu* (the *Complete Library of the Four Branches of Literature*) was a large book collection compiled in the Qing Dynasty (1616-1911), covering a time span of over 2,000 years from pre-Qin period to Qianlong Emperor's reign. The compilation was personally supervised by Qianlong Emperor (1711-1799). More than 360 renowned scholars and officials, including the famous scholar Ji Yun, were involved in compiling and editing the works and another 4,200 scholars participated in transcription. The project took 15 years to complete (1773-1787). The collection contains over 3,500 important works, with a total of 79,300 manuscript rolls in 36,000 volumes, and about 800 million characters. It is the largest collection of books in ancient China.

The collection is divided into four parts according to the ancient Chinese book classification convention: Classics, History, Works by Renowned Scholars, and Anthologies. Hence, it is called the *Complete Library of the Four Branches of Literature*. The Classics branch contains Confucian classics and related works; the History section features history books; classified under Works by Renowned Scholars are works of various schools of thought; and the Anthologies section includes collections of poetry, prose, and other literary works. The covers of the four sections are in green, red, blue, and taupe respectively, following the order of the seasons — spring, summer, autumn and winter — for ease of reference. To better preserve and disseminate these classics, seven extra copies were made

部，分别收藏于中国各地藏书阁。历经历史沧桑，全书现仅存文渊阁本、文津阁本、文溯阁本、文澜阁本四部全本。

《四库全书》保存了大量古代文献，内容覆盖哲学、历史、文艺、政治、社会、经济、军事、法律、医学、天文、地理、算学、生物学、农业、占卜等，系统呈现了中国古典文化的知识体系，是研究中国传统文化的重要文献。

and stored in libraries across China. Only four of these copies - those stored in the Wenyuan Ge (in the Palace Museum), the Wenjin Ge (in the Chengde Mountain Resort), the Wensu Ge (in Shenyang Imperial Palace) and the Wenlan Ge (the Imperial Library in Hangzhou) - have survived years of vicissitude.

The *Siku Quanshu* contains an enormous number of ancient texts, covering philosophy, history, culture and art, politics, society, the economy, military affairs, law, medicine, astronomy, arithmetic, biology, agriculture, and divination. It presents China's ancient culture in a systematic way, as an important window into traditional Chinese culture.

政治和社会制度

Political and Social Systems

自古以来，作为一个历史悠久的文明古国，中国逐渐积累起一系列有效的政治和社会制度，不仅维系了国家内部的团结和稳定，而且被周边国家和民族学习和借鉴，并对亚洲以外地区的社会发展产生了积极影响。尽管这些传统制度不能原封不动地迁移到现代社会，但经过创造性转化和创新性发展，它们仍然能够为当代中国国家和社会治理提供丰富的历史经验和文明智慧。

Over the course of its long history, China developed effective political and social systems which helped maintain unity and stability and provided models for its neighbors. They even had a positive impact on social development beyond Asia. Although they cannot be directly applied to any modern society, these ancient systems reveal ancient wisdom in governance and, through creative transformation and innovative development, can be used to respond to some of today's needs.

大一统

“大一统”出自《春秋公羊传》。“大”原指“尊崇”。“大一统”原意强调王者的权威，进而形成维护政治秩序稳定的向心力，同时，王者并不能恣意妄为，必须遵循天道的约束，才能获得统治的合法性。此外，“大一统”还强调中国的疆域版图范围须纳入统一的中央政府管辖之下。

“大一统”思想阐发了封建统治者的治理理念和政治追求，成为贯穿中国古代政治格局和思想文化的一条主线，深刻影响了中华民族共同体发展路向和中华民族多元一体演进格局。秦始皇（前259—前210）建立了第一个郡县制的大一统国家，奠定了中国古代政治的基本架构，开启了中国统一的多民族国家发展历程。此后，无论哪个民族入主中原，都以统一天下为己任，以中华文化的正统自居，深化了六合同风、四海一家的大一统传统。汉、唐、元、明、清是比较

Grand Unity

The term "grand unity" comes from the Gongyang Commentary on the Spring and Autumn Annals, where the word "grand" was originally used to highlight the importance of "respecting" unity. The term was used to emphasize the need to uphold the authority of the monarch in order to safeguard stability and the political order, and the need for the ruler to refrain from acting recklessly and respect the natural laws to secure the legitimacy of his rule. The term also emphasized that all Chinese territories must fall under the jurisdiction of a unified central government.

The concept of "grand unity" built on the governance theories and political goals of feudal rulers, and informed ancient China's political philosophy and culture. This idea guided the development of the Chinese nation towards a unified multi-ethnic community. Qinshihuang (259-210 B.C.), the first emperor of the Qin Dynasty (221-206 B.C.), unified China into a centralized state divided into commanderies and counties, a move that prepared the ground for ancient China's basic political structure, placing China on track to become a unified multi-ethnic state. From that point on every ruler of the Central Plains, regardless of their ethnic origin, took on the responsibility of protecting the unity of the entire country and claimed to be the true guardian of the Chinese traditions and culture. This continuity helped cement the concept of "grand unity" in the national psyche. The way the Han (206 B.C. - A.D. 220), Tang (618-907), Yuan (1206-1368), Ming (1368-1644), and Qing

典型的大一统王朝。历史多次证明，只要中国维持“大一统”的局面，国家就能够强盛、安宁、稳定，人民就会幸福安康。

大一统传统追求疆域领土的统一，推崇中央政府的权威，注重文化共识的凝聚。古代中国尽管经历多次分裂，但总能重新统一，主要原因就在于大一统观念塑造了中国人对“中国”的历史文化认同。漫长的大一统传统锻造出中央政府在各个地区间强有力的统筹协调能力，能够在广袤疆域内对各种人财物资源进行最大限度的优化配置，推动中国逐渐成为一个兼具多样性、包容性、稳定性的超大规模共同体。

(1616-1911) dynasties ruled typically reflects the idea of "grand unity". History has repeatedly shown that "grand unity" begets prosperity, peace, stability, and happiness.

"Grand unity" emphasized territorial unity, respect for the authority of the central government, and cultural cohesion. Ancient China did go through multiple periods of division, but they always culminated in reunification, mainly thanks to the role the concept of grand unity played in shaping the Chinese identity built into the Chinese people's historical and cultural consciousness. The long-standing tradition of grand unity gave the central government strong planning and coordination capabilities to optimize the allocation of personnel, resources, and materials across the vast territory, gradually making China a super large and inclusive community that embraced diversity and enjoyed stability.

宗法制

宗法制是产生于西周时期的一种权力继承制度，旨在将君位的传承用嫡长子继承制的形式确定下来，防止贵族之间因为权力继承问题发生纷争。宗法制等级森严，尊卑有序，以血缘关系为纽带，以君臣关系为纲纪，保证了贵族在政治上的垄断和特权地位，维护贵族统治集团内部的稳定和团结。

宗法制的积极作用是造成中华文化重视家庭建设，强调家庭伦理，形成了家庭强大的凝聚力。在宗法制影响之下，中国的宗族主要以家族方式体现，祠堂、家谱、族权的制度建设与之配套，形成浓厚的祖先崇拜传统，成为中国传统文化心理的一个重要特征。

Feudal Clan System

The feudal clan system, originating from the Western Zhou (1046-771 B.C.) period, governed the succession of power to ensure that the monarch was to be succeeded by his eldest son and prevent disputes among royal family members and nobles over the succession of power. The system was highly and strictly structured based on blood ties with a clear distinction between superior and inferior ranks. It was bound by kinship ties and governed by a master-servant relationship, which ensured the political monopoly and privileged position of the aristocracy, as well as the stability and unity of the ruling elite.

In terms of any positive effect of the feudal clan system on Chinese culture, we may highlight its emphasis on the importance of family and the development of family ethics. Under the influence of this system, Chinese families strengthened family cohesion by building ancestral shrines, developing genealogies, and exercising family authority, giving rise to a rich tradition of ancestor worship, which became an important feature of traditional Chinese culture.

郡县制

郡县制起源于春秋时期，秦始皇统一六国后正式推行全国，秦汉以后成为地方最基础的行政管理制度。郡，是在中央政府管理下的最高一级的地方行政机构，设郡守为最高行政长官。县，是郡的下级行政机构，设县令为最高行政长官。县、郡、中央政府与皇帝之间等级分明，构成了一个金字塔式的权力结构。在郡县制中，中央垂直管理地方，地方行政长官由皇帝直接任免，并在一定任期内进行流换。郡县制从根本上改变了西周以来分封割据的状况，打破了贵族势力对政府职务的垄断，成为官僚政治取代贵族政治的标志，对于加强中央集权，维护国家统一具有重要意义。

郡县制是大一统国家的制度基石，推动古代大一统国家

Political Subdivision: Commanderies and Counties

Division into commanderies and counties can be traced back to the Spring and Autumn period (770-476 B.C.). However, it was not until Qinshihuang conquered the other six states that the idea of political subdivision was officially implemented nationwide. Commanderies and counties emerged as dominant units of local government after the Qin (221-206 B.C.) and Han (206 B.C. - A.D. 220) dynasties. The commandery, headed by the governor, was the highest level of local government under the central government. Administrative divisions under a commandery were called counties, headed by county magistrates. This hierarchical relationship between counties, commanderies, the central government, and the emperor constituted a pyramid-like power structure. In this structure, the central government vertically oversaw local affairs and exercised oversight over the performance of local officials, and local chief administrators were appointed and removed directly by the emperor and might be subject to rotation. The introduction of this structure fundamentally changed the landscape of local government dominated by self-contained, separate fiefdoms that had existed since the Western Zhou Dynasty (1046-771 B.C.), and broke the aristocracy's monopoly of government positions. It heralded the emergence of the bureaucratic class in place of the aristocracy and was crucial to strengthening centralization and maintaining national unity.

This political subdivision system provided an institutional basis for "grand unity" in ancient China that led to the

的建立。郡县制对中国地方行政制度影响深远，中国现行的行政区划制度就是在传统郡县制的基础上演变和发展来的。

establishment of a unified country. It has had a far-reaching impact on China's local administration, and China's current administrative division system has evolved from its ancient predecessor.

行省制

行省制是中国古代一种行政制度，以省为最高一级的地方行政机构，反映了中国行政制度发展史上的重大变化。行省制起源于元朝，是当时中央与地方权力结构不断调整、完善以适应统一多民族国家治理要求的产物。

行省制确立了行省作为中央与地方关系的枢纽，是以中央集权为主，辅以部分地方分权的新体制，进一步削弱了地方政治、经济、文化的分离割据力量，加强了中央对地方的有效控制与管理，促进了国家统一和民族融合。这一制度奠定了元朝及以后中国地方行政管理制度和行政区域划分的整体结构，对后世乃至当代中国行政体制都产生了很大影响。

Political Subdivision: Provinces

Provinces were later established as the highest level of local government in ancient China in a significant change in China's administrative system. They were first created in the Yuan Dynasty (1206-1368) in response to a dynamic process of adjustment and improvement of the central and local power structures to meet the need to govern a unified multi-ethnic country.

Provinces served as a pivot of the central-local relationship, reliant on centralized administration with some degree of authority ceded to the local level. This helped reduce the possibility of local lords becoming too powerful politically, economically or culturally and tempted to build their own power bases insulated from outside interventions, and greatly strengthened control by the central government over the regions, which contributed to national unity and ethnic integration. The establishment of provinces defined an overall framework for China's local administration and administrative divisions during the Yuan Dynasty and beyond, and has had a great impact on later generations and even today.

科举制

科举制创立于隋朝，在1300多年的发展进程中不断调整、补充、更新、完善，形成了一套通过考试选拔官员的制度体系，成为中国古代最具特色与文化象征意义的政治选官制度。科举考试内容主要是儒家经典。

科举制把读书、考试和做官联系起来，让广大中下层社会人士有了通过读书考试改变命运的机会，是封建社会时期所可能采取的最公平的人才选拔形式，扩展了封建国家引进人才的社会层面，极大地促进了中国古代文化的发展。历史上，不仅有外国学子来中国参加科举考试，还有周边国家和欧美国家学习效仿中国这套“自由竞争、公开考试、平等竞争、择优取士”的选人制度，以建立本国的文官制度。

Imperial Civil Examination System

The Imperial Civil Examination System began in the Sui Dynasty (581-618) as a means of selecting officials through examinations. The system underwent constant adjustments, supplements, updates, and improvements over a span of 1,300 years. It became a defining characteristic of ancient China's cultural and political landscape. The examinations mainly focused on the Confucian classics.

The system established a link between education, examinations, and ascendance to officialdom, making it possible for people in the middle and lower classes to move up the social ladder. It was the fairest form of talent selection that existed in the feudal period. It expanded the talent pool and provided a great boost to the development of ancient Chinese culture. There were also foreign scholars traveling to China to take the examinations. Some neighboring countries and Western countries incorporated elements of China's system into their own screening processes for selecting civil servants, such as free and fair competition open to all, and merit-based selection.

三公九卿制

三公九卿制是秦汉时期形成的中央政府组织架构，是中国古代封建社会的一种官员制度。三公九卿制早在夏朝就已初具规模。秦朝建立封建统一国家后综合列国官僚制度，在中央政府建立起了完备的三公九卿制。

“三公九卿”是中央政府高级官员的统称。“三公”是最尊显的三个官职的合称，即掌管行政的丞相、掌管军事的太尉和负责监察的御史大夫，其代表中国传统以行政为主导的行政、军事、监察三权分立政治体制。“九卿”是各职能部门的长官，不一定是九个人或九种官职，意味着其官职完备。这一官员制度一直沿用到两晋南北朝时期，直至隋文帝在其结构基础上创设三省六部制，三公九卿制才退出历史舞台。

The system of Three Lords and Nine Ministers

The System of Three Lords and Nine Ministers was a central government organizational structure that emerged in the Qin and Han dynasties (221 B.C. - A.D. 220) in imperial China. The system took shape as early as the Xia Dynasty (c. 2100 B.C. - 1600 B.C.). When a unified feudal country was established by the First Emperor of Qin, the bureaucratic systems of previous states were integrated into a complete System of Three Lords and Nine Ministers for the central government.

The "Three Lords and Nine Ministers" were senior officials in the central government. The "Three Lords" were the Prime Minister, the Grand Marshal, and the Imperial Counsellor, the three most esteemed official positions. Respectively responsible for administration, military affairs, and oversight, they represented the separation of powers in the traditional Chinese political system with administration playing the primary role. The "Nine Ministers" were the heads of functional departments. The number of functional departments – and hence of ministers – was not necessarily nine. The number "nine" suggested a complete set of official posts. This system remained in place during the Jin Dynasty (265-420) and the Southern and Northern dynasties (420-581) until it was replaced with the System of Three Departments and Six Ministries, which Emperor Wendi of the Sui Dynasty (581-618) created based on this old structure.

三省六部制

三省六部制是中国古代封建社会的一套中央行政体制，三省和六部是其中的中枢权力机构和权力执行机构的总称。三省六部制确立于隋朝，完善于唐朝，不同时期的封建统治者为加强君主专制曾进行调整和补充。

“三省”代指中央政府，分别是中书省、门下省、尚书省。其中，中书省作为中央政策、文书的制定机构，负责以皇帝名义草拟制定官方文书；门下省作为中央最重要的文书审核机构，负责审查诏令，签署章奏，有权驳回；尚书省作为中央最高的行政事务管理机构，负责朝廷政令的执行。尚书省下设“六部”，分别为吏部、户部、礼部、兵部、刑部、工部，分工处理具体政务。三省六部职责明确，互相牵制，履行国家不同职能。作为一套组织严密的中央行政体制，三省六部制集中体现了中国古人的管理智慧，成为后来中国历史上的一项重要政治制度。

The System of Three Departments and Six Ministries

The System of Three Departments and Six Ministries was a central administrative system in imperial China. The departments and ministries refer to the authorities responsible for exercising power. The system was established in the Sui Dynasty (581-618) and improved during the Tang Dynasty (618-907), with subsequent feudal rulers making adjustments to reinforce their autocratic monarchy.

The "Three Departments" – the Central Secretariat, the Chancellery, and the Department of State Affairs – constituted the central government. The Central Secretariat drafted official documents on behalf of the emperor. The Chancellery was in charge of reviewing imperial edicts and signing off memorials to the throne and had the power to reject any documents. The Department of State Affairs, the highest administrative body responsible for implementing imperial decrees, had the "Six Ministries" under its direction, which each handled a specific brief – personnel management, finance, rites, the military, justice, and public works. With their responsibilities clearly defined, the Three Departments and Six Ministries checked and balanced one another in carrying out the functions of the state. This well-organized central administrative structure, which reflects ancient Chinese people's wisdom in governance, played an essential role as a political system in China's history.

古代监察制

中国古代监察制度是中国古代封建国家为监督政府官员，维护统治秩序，保证国家机器正常运转而设立的国家监督制度。中国古代监察机构和官员的主要职责包括监督法律、法令的实施，维护国家法律、法令的统一，参与、监督中央和地方司法机关对重大案件的审理等。

中国古代监察制度萌芽于先秦时期。秦汉是监察制度的创立阶段，并为其后历代王朝提供了仿效和演绎的基础。唐朝形成了传统监察制度较为完备的形态。历经宋元并于明清时期，中国古代监察制度达到顶峰。明朝大力加强监察权力的集中统一运用，形成了都察院制度，清代还制定了中国古代最完备的一部监察法典《钦定台规》。中国古代监察制度是传统大一统国家治理的重要基础和支撑，为当代监察制度的理论与实践提供了重要参考和依据。

Ancient Oversight System

The oversight system in ancient China was established as part of the feudal state system to oversee government officials, maintain social order, and ensure the orderly functioning of the state. The oversight institutions and officials were responsible for monitoring the implementation of laws and regulations, maintaining the coherence of state laws and regulations, and participating in and supervising the handling of major cases by central and local judicial authorities.

The origins of the ancient Chinese oversight system can be traced back to the pre-Qin period (770-221 B.C.). The system was formally established during the Qin and Han dynasties (221 B.C. - A.D. 220), and it provided a model for later dynasties to follow with necessary adjustments. It became a well-structured system in the Tang Dynasty (618-907), underwent further improvements in the Song and Yuan dynasties (960-1368), and reached its peak in the Ming and Qing dynasties (1368-1911). The Ming rulers centralized the power of oversight by establishing the Censorate. The Qing court enacted the *Qin Ding Tai Gui*, the most complete ancient Chinese oversight code. The system played an important role in the governance of ancient China, and can serve as an important reference framework for modern oversight theories and practices.

编户齐民

编户齐民是中国古代一种户籍制度，它产生于战国时期，规定政府管辖下的人都必须按姓名、年龄、籍贯等项目编入户籍。

西周时期，地方上的土地与人口归“宗族长”所有与管理。战国时期，各诸侯国为求富强，通过有效管理人口来增加税收，开始设置户籍制度，被编入户籍的百姓叫作“编户”。同时，各诸侯国开始直接管辖地方土地与人口，规定百姓都是国君的臣民，即“齐民”。两者总称“编户齐民”。

编户齐民既是行政管理制度，又是赋税制度。编户齐民具有独立的身份，其所承担的赋税和应服的徭役、兵役都与资产相关，同时在法律上拥有平等的地位。

Household Registration System

Ancient China's household registration system emerged during the Warring States period (475-221 B.C.). The system required anyone under the government's jurisdiction to register their name, age, and place of origin.

In the Western Zhou Dynasty (1046-771 B.C.), the head of each clan was responsible for managing anything related to the land and population in their local area. However, during the Warring States period, various feudal states sought to increase their wealth and power. To achieve this goal, a household registration system was established to effectively manage their populations and collect taxes. Those who were registered under the system were referred to as "registered households". In their attempt to directly govern matters related to local land and populations, the states rolled out rules stipulating that all people were subjects of the ruler and should be registered under the category of "common people".

In addition to being an administrative tool, the system helped collect taxes. The common people categorized under the registration system were considered to have independent identities, and were responsible for paying taxes and/or providing corvée labor or military service, based on their assets. They were equal before the law.

家谱

家谱是以表格、谱系、编年等形式记载家族世代相承的系统信息的文献，它记录了家族的繁衍和重要人物事迹，是中国古代宗法制度的产物，也是中国特有的历史文化遗产。

家谱是一个家族共同建构的集体记忆，不仅记载着一个家族的源流和迁徙过程，还涵盖了该家族繁衍、婚姻、文化、族规等历史文化的全记录。在社会功能上，家谱还具有区分家族成员血缘关系亲疏远近的作用。编修家谱是同姓同族人之间的大事，其目的主要是践行儒家重视血缘关系的思想，使族人世系明晰、长幼有序、尊敬祖宗、和睦亲善。

家谱是中华民族珍贵的文献资料，对于历史学、民俗学、人口学、社会学和经济学等各领域的学术研究，具有不可替代的独特作用。

Genealogy

A genealogy records systematic information about a family's lineage in the form of tables, family trees, and chronological accounts. It documents the reproduction of the family and the deeds of important individuals. A product of the feudal clan system in ancient China, it is a unique element of cultural heritage.

A genealogy represents a family's collective memories about its origin and migrations along with its entire historical and cultural legacy, including births, marriages, culture, and family rules. Genealogies also play a social function in distinguishing the degree of kinship between family members. Among people sharing the same surname or clan, compiling genealogies is a major activity with the primary aim of strengthening a sense of kinship as advocated by Confucian teachings, clarifying family lineages, establishing generational order, promoting respect for ancestors, and fostering harmony and affinity among family members.

Genealogies are invaluable documents. They play a unique and irreplaceable role in academic research across various fields, including history, folk-lore, demography, sociology, and economics.

五礼

中国是礼仪之邦，“礼”是中国传统文化的核心价值观念。西周时期，传统礼仪文化不断完备，其礼仪制度《周礼》将内容繁复的礼仪划分为“五礼”，即吉礼、嘉礼、宾礼、军礼、凶礼。汉代以后的礼仪制度虽有演进和变化，但基本上仍然围绕“五礼”进行建设。

吉礼是五礼之首，主要是对天神、地祇、人鬼的祭祀典礼。嘉礼指节庆活动等具有喜庆意义的礼仪，主要用于君主登基、节日受朝贺、公侯大夫士婚礼、冠礼、宴飨、乡饮酒礼等。宾礼是接待宾客的礼仪活动，包括读书人相见的

Five sets of rites

China is a nation of etiquette, and rites are at the core of traditional Chinese culture. During the Western Zhou Dynasty (1046-771 B.C.), traditional etiquette was refined and its guidebook, the "Rites of Zhou", categorized elaborate ceremonial etiquette into five sets of rites: the auspicious rites, the congratulatory rites, the hospitality rites, the military rites, and the inauspicious rites. While the system evolved after the Han Dynasty (206 B.C. - A.D. 25), China's ritual system continued to center around these five sets of rites.

The first set of rites, that is, the auspicious rites, involved offering sacrifices to heaven, the earth, and various spirits. The congratulatory rites dictated the way ceremonial events were held, such as enthronements, homage to rulers at festivals, marriages of nobles, capping rites for young males, royal banquets, and community gatherings with rural elders. The hospitality rites were about welcoming guests, including the etiquette for

◀作揖礼
Fist-and-palm salute

礼仪、邦交国之间的外交往来等。军礼是指古代军事活动方面的礼仪，例如召集和整顿军队，修筑城池，整修疆界、道路、沟渠等。凶礼是与丧葬、灾难相关的礼节。包括哀悼死亡的丧礼，哀吊灾祸的吊礼、抚恤遭受不幸时他国的恤礼等。“五礼”确立了古代礼仪制度的基本结构，对封建社会历代礼制产生深远影响。

hosting scholars and conducting diplomatic exchanges between allies. The military rites referred to the ritual practices related to ancient military activities, such as summoning and organizing troops, constructing city walls, and repairing boundaries, roads, and ditches. The inauspicious rites were related to funerals and disasters, including mourning the dead, offering condolences for victims of disasters, and showing sympathy for other states in times of misfortune. Together, these five sets of rites provided a basic framework for the ancient ritual system and had a profound influence on subsequent ritual practices in feudal society.

科学技术

Science and Technology

古代中国虽然没有独立发展出现代意义上的科学，但是在科技方面取得了巨大的成就。不论是天文学、数学，还是农业、手工业，都有很多重要成果流传至今。凝聚手工业智慧的瓷器（china），成为中国（China）一词译文的直接来源。特别是源远流长的中医，以其独树一帜的思维方式和诊疗手段，长期守护中华民族的健康福祉。中国古代科技根植于“天人合一”“道法自然”的智慧理念，为当今世界繁荣发展和人类文明进步提供了诸多启示。

Ancient China achieved great progress in science and technology, though it did not develop science in a modern sense. Many important achievements in astronomy, mathematics, agriculture, and handicraft-making are still relevant today. Porcelain, which embodies the skills of ancient Chinese craftsmen, was named "china" after the country. Traditional Chinese medicine, with its unique methods of diagnosis and treatment, has long contributed to the health and well-being of the Chinese people. Rooted in a philosophy that emphasizes "harmony between man and nature" and "the divine law that follows nature", ancient Chinese science and technology provide inspiration for global prosperity and the progress of human civilization.

四大发明

中国古代四大发明，即指南针、造纸术、印刷术、火药。四大发明是中国古代文明的标志性成就，对人类文明进程产生了深远影响。

指南针是用以判别方位的一种仪器。早在战国时期，中国人根据天然磁石指示南北的特性制成了“司南”，这是世界上最早的指南仪器。两宋时期，人们发明了用人工磁化铁针制成指南针的方法，并广泛应用于航海。12世纪末至13世纪初，指南针传入阿拉伯和欧洲，为欧洲航海家探索新航路提供了重要条件。

纸与人类日常生活息息相关。在纸发明之前，中国人曾把贝壳、兽骨、竹片、木片、丝绸等作为记录文字的载体。西汉初年，中国人发明了造纸术。1986年出土的西汉文帝时期的纸质地图残片，是迄今发现的人类社会最早的纸。东汉时期，蔡伦改进了造纸术。3至4世纪，纸成为中国最主要的书写材料。从4世纪末开始，造纸术逐渐传往朝鲜、日本，后经阿拉伯、埃及传入欧洲。造纸术是人类书写材料的

Four Great Inventions

The Four Great Inventions of ancient China were the compass, paper-making, printing, and gunpowder. These were hallmark achievements of ancient Chinese civilization that had a profound impact on the progress of human civilization.

The compass is an instrument used to determine direction. As early as the Warring States period (475-221 B.C.), the Chinese invented the "Si Nan" spoon compass, based on a natural magnet's ability to point to the north and the south. This was the world's earliest form of compass. In the Song Dynasty (960-1279), people made compasses with artificially magnetized iron needles, which were widely used in navigation. Between the late 12th century and the early 13th century, the compass was introduced to the Arab world and Europe, enabling European navigators to explore new routes.

Paper is closely related to daily life. Before its invention, the Chinese used shells, animal bones, bamboo and wooden slips, silk, and other materials for writing. Papermaking was invented in the early the Western Han Dynasty (206 B.C. - A.D. 25). Unearthed in 1986, a fragment of a paper map dating back to the time of Emperor Wendi of the Western Han Dynasty is the earliest known piece of paper. During the Eastern Han Dynasty (A.D. 25-220), Cai Lun improved the papermaking process. Between the 3rd and the 4th century, paper became the most important writing material in China. From the late 4th century, the art of papermaking spread to Korea and Japan, and later to Europe through the Arab world, especially Egypt.

伟大革命，有力促进了文化的保存和传播。

中国古代印刷术分为雕版印刷和活字印刷两个阶段。唐代发明的雕版印刷术，是把图文刻在木板上用水墨印刷，其前身是印章捺印和拓印碑石等。北宋时期，毕昇发明的活字印刷术，主要使用胶泥活字降低印刷成本同时提高效率，这比德国谷腾堡（1398—1468）的铅活字印刷术早约400年。宋元时期，中国出现了套色印刷技术。印刷术发明后，向东传到朝鲜、日本，向西经由阿拉伯传播到非洲和欧洲，为欧洲科学发展和文艺复兴运动提供了重要物质条件。

火药起源于炼丹术，是隋唐时期炼丹家发明的一种黑色或棕色的炸药。唐代中期已经有关于火药制作的记载。唐代末年，火药开始被运用于军事，出现了火炮、火箭等新式武器；到了宋朝，火器普遍用于军事战斗。火药经印度传入阿

Papermaking was a milestone in the development of writing materials, which effectively facilitated the preservation and dissemination of culture.

Ancient Chinese printing technology underwent two stages: woodblock printing and movable type printing. Woodblock printing, invented in the Tang Dynasty (618-907), was a process of printing texts and images with ink by first carving them onto wooden blocks. This technique had its roots in seal engraving and rubbing copies of inscriptions on stone tablets. During the Northern Song Dynasty (960-1127), Bi Sheng invented movable typeset printing. His method used movable clay type pieces, which reduced costs and increased efficiency. This invention appeared 400 years earlier than Johannes Gutenberg's movable metal typeset printing in Germany. During the Song and Yuan dynasties (960-1368), China developed multi-color printing. Ancient China's printing technology spread eastward to Korea and Japan and westward via the Arab world to Africa and Europe, paving the way for the development of science and the Renaissance in Europe.

Gunpowder, a black or brown explosive substance derived from alchemy, was invented in the Sui and Tang dynasties (581-907). There are records of gunpowder production from the middle of the Tang Dynasty. By the end of the Tang Dynasty, gunpowder was being used for military purposes, leading to the development of new weapons such as cannons and rockets. By the time of the Song Dynasty (960-1279), firearms were

拉伯国家，再传到欧洲乃至世界各地。火药兵器逐步取代了冷兵器，在战争战术、攻城筑城等技术发展和社会进步方面产生了革命性影响，推动了世界历史发展的进程。

commonly used in battles. Gunpowder spread to Arab countries via India and then to Europe and other parts of the world. Firearms gradually replaced cold weapons and had a revolutionary impact on war tactics and fortification construction, and many other aspects of technological and social development, accelerating the progress of human civilization.

二十八宿

二十八宿是中国古代对黄道附近二十八组星象的总称。中国古人为便于观测日、月和金、木、水、火、土五星的方位，将黄道附近的星象划分为二十八组，作为观测天象的坐标，类似于现代天文学中的星座。目前已知二十八宿完整名称的最早记载，出现在湖北随县出土的战国时期曾侯乙墓中。

“宿”即日、月、五星的栖息之地。二十八宿分为四组，东、南、西、北各七宿。每个方位的七宿连缀起来与四种动物的外形相似，称为“四象”，即东方青龙、南方朱雀、西方白虎、北方玄武。

二十八宿是中国古人关于星空划分体系的基本知识，是中国古代天文学的重要内容。作为中国传统文化的重要标识，二十八宿曾被广泛应用于古代天文、宗教、文学、星占、风水等领域，具有丰富多样的文化内涵。

Twenty-Eight Mansions

The Twenty-Eight Mansions is a general term for the twenty-eight groups of stars near the ecliptic. To help observe the positions of the sun, the moon, Venus, Jupiter, Mercury, Mars, and Saturn, the ancient Chinese divided the stars near the ecliptic into twenty-eight groups, which served as coordinates for observing celestial phenomena, similar to constellations in modern astronomy. The earliest known record of the complete names of the Twenty-Eight Mansions was discovered in the Tomb of the Marquis Yi of Zeng, unearthed in Suixian County, Hubei Province, which dates back to the Warring States period (475-221 B.C.).

The mansions are the dwelling places of the sun, the moon, and the five planets. The Twenty-Eight Mansions were divided into four sections based on their directions. The seven mansions in each section, when linked together, resemble the shape of an animal. The four animals – the Azure Dragon of the East, the Vermilion Bird of the South, the White Tiger of the West, and the Black Tortoise of the North – were known as the "Four Mythological Symbols".

The concept of the Twenty-Eight Mansions underpinned the understanding of the constellations in ancient China and constitutes an integral part of ancient Chinese astronomy. As an important symbol of traditional Chinese culture with rich and diverse cultural meanings, the concept was widely used in ancient China in areas such as astronomy, religion, literature, divination, and feng shui.

天干地支

天干地支简称“干支”，是中国古代天文历法的基本计数单位，源自中国远古时代对天象的观测。“干”原指树干，“支”原指树枝。天干有十个，依次为：甲、乙、丙、丁、戊、己、庚、辛、壬、癸；地支有十二个，依次为：子、丑、寅、卯、辰、巳、午、未、申、酉、戌、亥。十天干和十二地支按固定的顺序相互配合，组成干支纪元法。干支纪元法是中国古人纪年、月、日、时的重要方法，直到现在仍是中国农历纪年的基本单位，例如，2022年是农历壬寅年，2023年是农历癸卯年。

中国民间又将十二地支与十二生肖（鼠、牛、虎、兔、龙、蛇、马、羊、猴、鸡、狗、猪）相配，与农历年相对应，如壬寅年为虎年，癸卯年为兔年。干支纪年法以六十年为一个周期，称为一“甲子”。这种纪年法反映了中国古人循环往复、生生不息的历史观。此外，天干地支还广泛应用于术数、计数、命名等领域。

Heavenly Stems and Earthly Branches

Heavenly stems and earthly branches (or Tian Gan Di Zhi, commonly abbreviated to Gan Zhi) are the basic units of the ancient Chinese astronomical calendar, which originated from the observation of celestial phenomena. "Gan" literally means stems and "Zhi" means branches. There are ten heavenly stems: Jia, Yi, Bing, Ding, Wu, Ji, Geng, Xin, Ren, and Gui, and twelve earthly branches: Zi, Chou, Yin, Mao, Chen, Si, Wu, Wei, Shen, You, Xu, and Hai. The heavenly stems and earthly branches are combined in a fixed order to form the Gan Zhi chronology, an important means of recording years, months, days, and hours in ancient China. They are still the basic units of the Chinese lunar calendar today. For example, 2022 is the year of Ren Yin with the heavenly stem "Ren" and the earthly branch "Yin", and 2023 is the year of Gui Mao with the heavenly stem "Gui" and the earthly branch "Mao".

In Chinese folk culture, the twelve earthly branches are paired with the twelve zodiac animals (rat, ox, tiger, rabbit, dragon, snake, horse, goat, monkey, rooster, dog, and pig). Each animal corresponds to a lunar year. For example, the year of Ren Yin is the year of the tiger, and the year of Gui Mao is the year of the rabbit. The Gan Zhi chronology is based on a 60-year cycle, known as a "Jia Zi", reflecting the ancient Chinese belief in the cyclical nature of history. It was also widely used in divination, arithmetic, naming, and other fields.

二十四节气

二十四节气是中国古人根据农业生产的需要，通过观察天体运行，认知一年中时令、气候、物候等变化规律所形成的知识体系，是中国农历的重要组成部分。

中国古人将一个太阳回归年分为春、夏、秋、冬四季，每季三个月，每月各两个节气。二十四节气分别为：立春、雨水、惊蛰、春分、清明、谷雨，立夏、小满、芒种、夏至、小暑、大暑，立秋、处暑、白露、秋分、寒露、霜降，立冬、小雪、大雪、冬至、小寒、大寒。

二十四节气准确反映了自然节律变化，在古代农耕社会发挥了极为重要的作用。其早在西汉时期就已被纳入历法，用于指导农业生产，并逐渐演化为包含丰富民俗文化含义的文化体系，成为中华文化的重要组成部分。

在古代，二十四节气传播到朝鲜、日本、越南等国家，对当地农耕生产和社会文化发展产生了积极影响。二十四节气因其科学性和准确性，受到国际气象界的认可与推崇。2016年，“二十四节气”列入联合国教科文组织人类非物质文化遗产代表作名录。

Twenty-Four Solar Terms

The Twenty-Four Solar Terms were developed in ancient China based on the observation of astronomical phenomena and the understanding of the changes in seasons, climate, and phenology, to meet the needs of agricultural production. They form an important part of the Chinese lunar calendar.

The ancient Chinese divided a solar year into four seasons, each with three months and each month with two solar terms. The Twenty-Four Solar Terms are: Start of Spring, Rain Water, Awakening of Insects, Vernal Equinox, Clear and Bright, Grain Rain, Start of Summer, Grain Full, Grain in Ear, Summer Solstice, Minor Heat, Major Heat, Start of Autumn, End of Heat, White Dew, Autumnal Equinox, Cold Dew, Frost Descent, Start of Winter, Minor Snow, Major Snow, Winter Solstice, Minor Cold, and Major Cold.

The solar terms accurately reflect the changes in nature and played a crucial role in ancient China's agricultural society. Included in the calendar as early as the Western Han Dynasty (206 B.C. - A.D. 25), they guided agricultural production and gradually became infused in folk traditions. They constitute an important part of Chinese culture.

The Twenty-Four Solar Terms spread to countries such as Korea, Japan, and Vietnam in ancient times, and had a positive influence on their agriculture and cultural development. The international meteorological community recognizes the scientific accuracy of the solar terms. In 2016, they were included on the UNESCO's Representative List of the Intangible Cultural Heritage of Humanity.

青铜器

青铜器是中国古代用铜、锡等合金经烧制、锻造后形成的各种器物，刚刚铸造完成时呈金色，但因为埋藏地下时间长久，青铜表面氧化，产生铜锈后变为青绿色，被称为“青铜”。

中国已知最古老的青铜器是甘肃马家窑文化遗址出土的青铜刀，距今约5000年。中国的青铜时代为夏、商、西周至春秋时期（公元前21世纪—公元前5世纪），其中商周时期的器物最为精美。商朝晚期到西周早期，青铜铸造技艺达到巅峰。商四羊青铜方尊是中国现存商代青铜方尊中最大的一件；商后母戊鼎是至今世界上出土的体量最大的青铜鼎，它们均代表了高度发达的商代青铜文化。

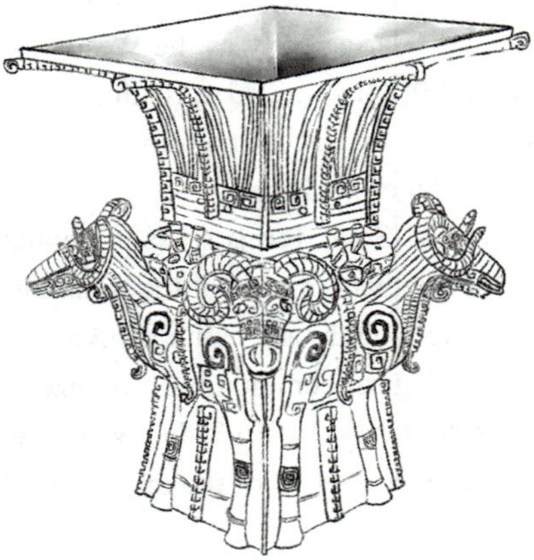

Bronzeware

Bronzeware refers to a variety of utensils crafted from an alloy comprised mainly of copper and tin that were cast and forged in ancient China. When freshly cast, bronze has a golden hue. However, over time, it acquires a greenish-blue patina, especially after being buried underground.

The oldest known item of Chinese bronzeware is a knife uncovered at the Majiayao culture site in Gansu province, dating back roughly 5,000 years. The Bronze Age (c. 2100 B.C. - c. 500 B.C.) in China spanned the Xia (c. 2070-1600 B.C.), Shang (1600-1046 B.C.), and Western Zhou (1046-771 B.C.) dynasties and the Spring and Autumn period (770-476 B.C.), with the bronzeware cast in the Shang and Zhou (1046-256 B.C.) dynasties being the best. Bronze casting reached its peak during the late Shang and early Zhou periods. The Siyang Fangzun, a square vessel with four goats, is the largest surviving bronze square vessel made during the Shang Dynasty, and the Simuwu Ding, a rectangular colossus with four legs, is the world's heaviest bronze item discovered to date. Both vessels represent a high level of development of the bronze-age culture during the Shang Dynasty.

◀ 商四羊青铜方尊
Siyang Fangzun, from Shang Dynasty

在中国古代，青铜器是国家政权的象征。在夏商周时期，青铜器主要作为祭祀的礼器，它的使用有繁复严格的等级规定，身份地位不同，所使用的青铜器数量和形制大小也不同。青铜器集中体现了中国古代生产技术和艺术发展的水平，在中国古代文明史中占有重要地位。

In ancient China, bronzeware was a symbol of state power and was primarily used as sacrificial vessels during the Xia, Shang, and Zhou dynasties. The utilization of bronzeware was subject to complex and strict regulations based on an individual's rank and status, and the number and size of items varied according to their social standing. Bronzeware reflects the level of technological and artistic development of ancient Chinese civilization. It holds an important position in the history of ancient Chinese culture.

浑天仪

浑天仪是中国古代观测天体运行的仪器，主要由浑仪和浑象构成。浑仪是测量天体球面坐标的一种仪器，浑象是古代用来演示天象的仪表。其理论基础是“浑天说”。该学说认为天是一个圆球，像鸡蛋，地球就像鸡蛋黄一样，立于其中，这是当时天文学说中先进的认识。

东汉天文学家张衡（78—139）在前人的基础上对浑天仪进行了重要改进，在117年制成一件铜铸浑天仪。据记载，其主体是一个由几层均可运转的圆圈组成的铜球，其中通过南北极的圆环叫子午圈，另一个是表示地平线的地平圈。各层分别刻着南、北极，黄、赤道，二十四节气，二十八列宿，日、月等天象。通过精妙的设计，铜球转动一周的速度和地球自转一周的速度相同，使得铜铸浑天仪能够实时模拟星空的运行。

浑天仪是中国古代天文学成就的杰出代表，对世界天文

Celestial Globe

The celestial globe is a device that was used in ancient China to observe the motion of celestial bodies. It is composed of two main observing devices: the armillary sphere and the celestial sphere. The armillary sphere measures the spherical coordinates of celestial bodies, while the celestial sphere demonstrates celestial phenomena. Its theoretical basis is the *huntianshuo*, a geocentric theory in ancient Chinese astronomy, that views the universe as a sphere, like an egg, with the Earth as the central yolk. That was a useful perspective back then.

Zhang Heng (78-139), an astronomer of the Eastern Han Dynasty (25 - 220) made significant improvements to the celestial globe based on the work of his predecessors. He created a copper celestial globe in 117. According to records, the main body of the celestial globe was a copper sphere surrounded by several layers of circles that could all rotate. The vertical circle passing through the North and South poles was called the celestial meridian, and another circle representing the horizon was called the horizon circle. On the surface of each layer were carved the South pole, the North pole, the equator, the ecliptic, the Twenty-Four Solar Terms, the twenty-eight mansions in astrology, the sun, the moon, and other celestial bodies. This ingenious design allowed the speed of the copper sphere's rotation to match that of the Earth's rotation, simulating the movement of the stars in real time.

The celestial globe is a remarkable product of ancient

学理论及实践产生了深远的影响。在17世纪望远镜发明之前，浑天仪是天文学家在测定天体方位时必不可少的仪器。

Chinese astronomy that had a profound impact on the world's astronomical theory and practice. Before the invention of telescopes in the 17th century, it was an essential instrument for astronomers to determine the position of celestial bodies.

《授时历》

《授时历》是中国古代的一种精确历法。1276年，元世祖忽必烈（1215—1294）要求许衡（1209—1281）与郭守敬（1231—1316）、王恂（1235—1281）共同研订新历法。为了编纂新历法，他们在全国范围内进行大规模天体测量，为修订历法提供精确数据。1280年，新历法编成，忽必烈将其取名为《授时历》，自1281年起颁行使用。

《授时历》打破了古代制历的传统，第一次把小数引入历法，以365.2425日为一回归年，与地球环绕太阳公转一周的实际时间仅差25.92秒，其精度与现行世界通用的公历相当，比西方早300多年，反映了当时中国天文历法的新水平。《授时历》是中国古代最先进、最精确、使用时间最长的历法，也是当时世界上最先进的一部历法，曾传播至日本、朝鲜、越南及欧洲等地，对当地的历法产生了深远影响。

Shoushi Calendar

The *Shoushi* Calendar was an accurate calendar in ancient China. In 1276, Kublai Khan (1215-1294), the first emperor of the Yuan Dynasty (1206-1368), tasked Xu Heng (1209-1281), Guo Shoujing (1231-1316) and Wang Xun (1235-1281) with creating a more precise calendar. To this end, these astronomers conducted nationwide observations to gather accurate data for the new calendar. By 1280, the calendar was completed and Kublai Khan named it the Shoushi Calendar, which came into use in 1281.

The *Shoushi* Calendar was groundbreaking in its adoption of a decimal time system. The system determined that the length of the tropical year was 365.2425 days, only 25.92 seconds off from the current measurement of a year. This level of accuracy is comparable to the widely used Gregorian Calendar, but the *Shoushi* Calendar was developed over 300 years earlier. The *Shoushi* Calendar is regarded as the most advanced, accurate, and long-lasting calendar in ancient China. It was also considered the most advanced calendar in the world at that time. Its influence extended far beyond China, as it spread to countries and regions such as Japan, Korea, Vietnam, and Europe, where it had a profound effect on their respective calendars.

《九章算术》

《九章算术》是中国汉唐之间出现的十部古算书《算经十书》中最重要的一部数学专著，成书于1世纪左右，西汉早期著名数学家张苍、耿寿昌等对它进行过增补删订。现今流传的主要是魏晋时期著名数学家刘徽（约225—约295）为《九章算术》所作的注本。

《九章算术》系统总结了自先秦时期到东汉时期的数学成就，全书共有九卷，包括方田、粟米、衰分、少广、商功、均输、盈不足、方程、勾股九个章节。全书采用问题集的形式，收录了246个生产、生活实践相关的应用问题，其中每道题都有答案和解题步骤，确定了中国古代数学以计算为中心、密切联系实际、解决实践问题的研究风格和框架。书中提到的负数、分数计算，联立一次方程解法等都是具有

The Nine Chapters on the Mathematical Art

The Nine Chapters on the Mathematical Art is the most important mathematical treatise among the 10 ancient books on mathematics that make up the *Ten Classics of Mathematics*,"which appeared in China between the Han (206 B.C. - A.D. 220) and Tang (618-907) dynasties. It can be traced back to around the 1st century, and renowned mathematicians such as Zhang Cang and Geng Shouchang in the early Western Han Dynasty (206 B.C. - A.D. 25) made additions and revisions to it. The version that has been passed down to this day is the annotated edition of "The Nine Chapters on the Mathematical Art" by Liu Hui (c. 225 – 295), an eminent mathematician in the Wei (220-265) and Jin (265-420) dynasties.

The Nine Chapters on the Mathematical Art systematically summarizes the mathematical achievements from the pre-Qin period (770-221 B.C.) to the Eastern Han period (25-220). The book consists of nine chapters – "Field Measurement", "On Millet and Rice", "Distribution by Proportion", "What Width?", "Construction Consultations", "Fair Levies", "Excess and Deficit", "The two-sided reference", and "Base and altitude". It is a how-to manual comprising 246 exemplary problems related to work and daily life, each with answers and steps to the solution. It offered a research model and framework for ancient Chinese mathematics with a focus on computation, practical relevance, and problem-solving. The methods offered in the book for calculating negative numbers and fractions and for solving simultaneous linear equations were mathematical

世界领先意义的数学成就，这些成就比印度早800年，比欧洲早1000余年。

《九章算术》是当时世界上最简练有效的应用数学成果，它的出现标志中国古代数学体系的形成，为中国古典数学领先世界奠定了基础。《九章算术》于隋唐时期传入朝鲜和日本，后传至印度、阿拉伯国家和欧洲地区，对世界古典数学发展产生了很大影响。

breakthroughs at that time, predating those of India by 800 years and Europe by more than 1,000 years.

A mathematical masterpiece, *The Nine Chapters on the Mathematical Art* offered concise explanations on effective solutions to problems in applied mathematics. It represented a high water mark for ancient China's understanding of mathematics, placing China on track to lead in the field of classical mathematics. The book was introduced to Korea and Japan during the Sui (581-618) and Tang dynasties before it made its way to India, Arab countries, and Europe, and exerted a great influence on the development of classical mathematics worldwide.

祖冲之

祖冲之（429—500）是南北朝时期杰出的数学家、天文学家。他一生钻研自然科学，在数学、天文历法和机械制造等方面都作出了卓越的贡献。

祖冲之首次将圆周率精算到小数点后第七位，即在3.1415926和3.1415927之间。他对圆周率数值的精确推算值，对于中国乃至世界是一个重大贡献，后人将“这个精确推算值”用他的名字命名为“祖冲之圆周率”。直到16世纪，这一精算纪录才被打破。此外，由祖冲之撰写的《大明历》是当时最科学、先进的历法。按照他的推算，一个回归年的长度和今时的推算值仅相差46秒，这为世界天文研究奠定了坚实基础。

为了纪念祖冲之对中国和世界科学文化作出的杰出贡献，紫金山天文台将1964年发现的国际永久编号为1888的小行星命名为“祖冲之星”。

Zu Chongzhi

Zu Chongzhi (429-500) was an outstanding mathematician and astronomer during the Northern and Southern dynasties (420-589). He devoted his life to the study of natural sciences and made remarkable contributions to mathematics, astronomy, calendrical calculations, and mechanical engineering.

Zu was the first to calculate the value of pi to an accuracy of seven decimal places, between 3.1415926 and 3.1415927, which was a major contribution to China and the world. His calculation of Pi was later named after him as "Zu Chongzhi's Pi", and this record in accuracy was not surpassed until the 16th century. In addition, the "Daming calendar" Zu compiled was the most accurate calendar at that time. His calculation of the length of a tropical year differs from the modern value by only 46 seconds; it laid solid foundations for astronomical research worldwide.

To celebrate Zu Chongzhi's remarkable contributions to science and culture, the Purple Mountain Observatory named an asteroid – which was discovered in 1964 and given the international permanent number 1888 – "Zu Chongzhi Star".

《黄帝内经》

中国传统医经名著《黄帝内经》，约成书于战国时期，是中国古代医学典籍的集大成者，也是一部重要的自然哲学著作。

《黄帝内经》原书十八卷，由《素问》和《灵枢》两部分组成。《素问》侧重于中医学理论，提出并阐述了阴阳学说、五行学说、运气学说、养生学说等内容；《灵枢》侧重于临床诊治，其论述重心是脏腑经络、针灸疗法等。该书以黄帝和岐伯等人对话的形式展开，在天人合一、形神统一、阴阳和平等中国传统哲学理念的指导下，深入论述了人与自然万物的关系，探讨了人的生理、病理以及疾病的诊断、治疗等问题。

《黄帝内经》系统总结了中国古代医学的临床经验和理论成就，完整建构了一套中医学理论体系。在古代，《黄帝内经》是日本、朝鲜等国学习中医的主要著作。直至今天，《黄帝内经》仍然是中医学研究必读的经典文献，并被译为多种语言，在世界医学界广泛传播。

Huangdi Neijing

The *Huangdi Neijing* is a classic of traditional Chinese medicine compiled during the Warring States period (475-221 B.C.). It is a comprehensive collection of ancient Chinese medical literature and an important work of natural philosophy.

The original collection consists of 18 volumes divided into two parts: *Suwen* and *Lingshu*. *Suwen* focuses on the theory of traditional Chinese medicine and presents and elaborates on various concepts such as yin and yang, the five elements, vital energy and wellness. *Lingshu* focuses on clinical diagnosis and treatment; its main discussions are on the internal organs, channels and collaterals, and acupuncture therapy.

The book, written in the form of a dialogue between Huangdi and Qibo, delves deeply into the relationship between humans and all other natural phenomena, guided by traditional Chinese philosophical concepts such as the unity of humanity and nature, the unity of form and spirit, and the balance of yin and yang. It also explores issues such as human physiology, pathology, diagnosis, and treatment of diseases.

The *Huangdi Neijing* is a comprehensive summary of the theoretical achievements and clinical experience in ancient Chinese medicine, representing a complete theoretical system of traditional Chinese medicine. In ancient times, it was the main text for studying traditional Chinese medicine in countries such as Japan and Korea. Even today, it remains a classic text that is essential for the study of traditional Chinese medicine. It has been translated into multiple languages, and widely circulates around the globe.

《伤寒论》

中医学经典著作《伤寒论》由东汉著名医学家张仲景（约150—154至约215—219）撰写。这一著作确立了“辨证施治”的治疗原则，论述了外感热病的病理、诊断、疗法、方剂，是中国医学史上第一部理、法、方、药俱备的经典著作。自宋代以后，这一著作受到历代医家的重视，对其整理、诠述、注释者多至数百家，大大提高了当时中医临床治疗水平。

《伤寒论》记载的方剂不但精于选药、讲究配伍，还可以针对病情发展灵活加减变化，经中国历代医家的反复应用，疗效显著，因此被后世誉为“众方之祖”，尊之为“经方”。

Shanghan Lun

The *Shanghan Lun*, a classic work of traditional Chinese medicine, was written by the renowned medical expert Zhang Zhongjing (c. 150-154 - c. 215-219) during the Eastern Han Dynasty (25-220). This work established the principle of "syndrome identification and treatment" and discussed the pathology of febrile diseases, their diagnosis, treatment methods, and prescription medications. It is the first classic work in the history of Chinese medicine that combines theory, diagnosis methodology, treatment, and medicine. Later medical experts, especially those after the Song Dynasty (960-1279), highly valued this work, and hundreds of scholars were involved in its editing, interpretation, and annotation, greatly improving clinical treatment at the time.

The standard prescriptions recorded in the *Shanghan Lun* reveal a high level of rigor in selecting and combining medicinal ingredients together with a degree of flexibility in adjusting medication to the development of a disease. These prescriptions were used by Chinese medical practitioners throughout history, and they showed significant therapeutic effects, and were thus hailed as a classic reference for doctors.

《本草纲目》

中国古代本草医药学经典《本草纲目》是明代著名医药学家李时珍（1518—1593）于1578年成书的中医药文献。全书190万余字，共分52卷，收载药物近2000种，记录药方10000余个，是中国现存最为系统全面、翔实完备的古代医药学典籍。

本草指代中药，是传统中医的主要药物，以植物药材居多。在中国医药学史上，《本草纲目》首次记载了大量本草药物的功效、主治、临床运用，是记载本草最多的中医药典籍，极大地扩充了中华本草的内容。书中首创本草分类方法，确立了科学的本草编目体系，在分类形式上推动中国古代本草开始向现代药物学发展。

Bencao Gangmu (*Compendium of Materia Medica*)

A classic of traditional Chinese medicine and pharmacology, *Ben Cao Gang Mu* was compiled by the renowned Ming Dynasty physician Li Shizhen (1518-1593) in 1578. The book is divided into 52 volumes with a total of over 1.9 million characters. It lists nearly 2,000 medicinal substances and over 10,000 recorded prescriptions. It is the most comprehensive and complete ancient medical and pharmacological work in China that has survived to the present day.

Bencao refers to Chinese herbal medicine. In the history of Chinese medicine, the compendium was the first and most comprehensive ancient medical text to record the efficacy and clinical uses of a large number of Chinese herbal medicines. Its publication greatly helped spread the knowledge of Chinese herbal medicine. The book established a scientific classification system for herbal medicine, which paved the way for the development of Chinese herbal medicine towards modern pharmacology.

◀中药 党参
Dang Shen (Pilose Asiabell root), an herb

《本草纲目》采用以药带方、以方附药的方式介绍本草和医方，既证实了药物功效，又加深了医者对药物的认识，具有很强的实用价值。《本草纲目》还是一本百科全书式的博物学著作，关联探讨了天文学、地理学、物理学、气象学等诸多学科的内容，对世界医药学、植物学、动物学、矿物学以及化学的发展产生了深远影响。

早在17世纪，《本草纲目》就已流传到海外，在日本、朝鲜等地引起广泛关注。这一典籍被陆续翻译为日文、法文、英文等多语种版本广泛传播，成为海外学者研究中医药、本草学、博物学等相关学科的重要文献。

The *Bencao Gangmu* introduces herbal medicines together with standard prescriptions. This is a highly practical approach that validates the effectiveness of the medicines and expands the understanding of them among medical professionals. The book is also an encyclopedic work in the field of natural history, and explores the subjects of astronomy, geography, physics, meteorology, and many other disciplines. It has had a profound impact on the development of world medicine, botany, zoology, mineralogy, chemistry, and other fields.

The *Bencao Gangmu* was introduced overseas in as early as the 17th Century and attracted widespread attention in Japan, Korea, and other countries. This classic work has been translated into multiple languages, including Japanese, French, and English, and has become an important reference for overseas scholars studying traditional Chinese medicine, materia medica, and natural history.

针灸

针灸是中医针刺疗法和艾灸疗法的总称，是中医治疗疾病、预防保健最常用的两种外治方法。这两种方法均是通过刺激经络、穴位，达到防病、治病的目的，在中医治疗保健中经常配合使用，故合称为针灸。

针刺疗法是用金属制成的细针，运用不同手法，刺入身体一定穴位，以一定的手法疏通经络、调理气血。艾灸疗法是点燃用艾绒搓成的艾条或艾炷，缓慢温熏人体穴位，借助艾条燃烧的温和热力、药物作用，温经散寒、温通气血。针灸疗法简便易行，疗效迅速显著，医疗成本较低，几乎没有副作用，而且可以协同其他疗法进行综合治疗。由于具有这些独特优势，长期以来，针灸疗法一直深受人们的认可。

早在唐代，中国针灸就已经传播到日本、朝鲜、越南等国家。截至目前，针灸已经传播到世界140多个国家和地区，为保障各国人民生命安全和身体健康发挥了重要作用，越来越多的人体验到了针灸的疗效和中医的神奇。

Acupuncture and moxibustion

Acupuncture and moxibustion are two forms of therapy in traditional Chinese medicine. They are the most commonly used external methods for disease prevention and treatment. Both methods act by stimulating the meridians and acupuncture points. They are often used in combination in traditional Chinese medicine and health care.

Acupuncture therapy involves the use of fine metal needles to stimulate specific acupuncture points on the body, utilizing various techniques to regulate the meridians and adjust the flow of qi and blood. Moxibustion therapy slowly warms specific acupuncture points on the body using moxa sticks or moxa cones made from compressed mugwort. The gentle heat and medicinal properties of moxibustion help to warm the meridians, alleviate cold symptoms, and enhance the circulation of qi and blood. Acupuncture and moxibustion therapy offers convenience, with rapid and significant effects at low medical cost and almost no side effects. Moreover, they can be used in conjunction with other therapies to provide comprehensive treatment. Due to these unique advantages, the value of acupuncture and moxibustion therapy has been widely recognized.

Acupuncture and moxibustion therapy was introduced to countries such as Japan, Korea and Vietnam as early as the Tang Dynasty (618-907). The therapy has now spread to over 140 countries and regions, and plays an important role in healthcare worldwide. More and more people have benefited from the therapeutic effects of acupuncture and the wonders of traditional Chinese medicine.

《齐民要术》

中国古代综合性农学专著《齐民要术》，由北魏农学家贾思勰撰写，约成书于北魏末年（533—544），是中国现存最早的一部完整的农书，被誉为“中国古代农业百科全书”。

《齐民要术》全书共10卷、92篇，正文7万多字，注释4万多字。这一著作强调农业的重要性，全面总结了6世纪以前黄河中下游地区劳动人民长期积累的农业生产经验、农产品加工和贮藏以及治荒的方法等，详细介绍了季节、气候、土壤与农作物的关系，强调农业生产要因时因地，因作物品种而采取不同办法。此外，书中重视对农业生产、科学技术和经济效益的综合分析，提倡改革生产技术和生产工具，总结了抗旱、恢复提高土壤肥力、选种育种等生产技术知识。

《齐民要术》不仅反映了古代中国领先于世的农业发展

Qimin Yaoshu (*Important Methods for the People's Welfare*)

Qimin Yaoshu (*Important Methods for the People's Welfare*), a monograph of agriculture-related topics in ancient China, was written by Northern Wei Dynasty agriculturalist Jia Sixie, between the late years of the Northern Wei Dynasty (386-534) and the early years of the Eastern Wei Dynasty (534-550). *Qimin Yaoshu* is the earliest agricultural text that is completely preserved in China, and it is crowned as "the encyclopedia of ancient Chinese agriculture."

Qimin Yaoshu comprises 10 scrolls, 92 chapters, with a total of over 70,000 Chinese characters, plus over 40,000 characters of annotations. The book emphasizes the importance of agriculture; it comprehensively summarizes the experience of peasants living in the middle and lower reaches of the Yellow River before the 6th century, including agricultural production experience, processing of agricultural products and methods for their storage, the way to open up wasteland and so on. The book tells how season, climate and soil affect the growth of crops, and emphasizes that different varieties of crop should grow in the right season, on right land and with right farming methods. In addition, the book sheds light on the comprehensive analysis of agricultural production, science and technologies as well as how more economic benefits can be created. It advocates improving technologies and production tools, and provides knowlege about fighting a drought, recovering land fertility, and seed selection and breeding.

This book not only tells about the advanced level and

水平，而且对后世农业发展和农业科学进步产生了深远影响。作为世界农学史上最早的专著之一，《齐民要术》先后传至日本、欧洲等地，成为海内外研究古物种变化的经典。

leading position of China's agriculture at the time but also has a far-reaching influence on the development of agriculture and agricultural science and technology. As one of the earliest agricultural monographs in global agriculture history, *Qimin Yaoshu* spread to other parts of the world including Japan and Europe, becoming a classic in the study of species variation.

《天工开物》

《天工开物》是世界上第一部关于农业和手工业生产的综合性著作，初刊于1637年，作者是明代科学家宋应星（1587—约1666）。该书涉及18个生产领域，记录了130多项生产技术和工具，并绘制123幅精美的插图进行生动呈现。

在农业方面，该书论述了土壤、气候条件以及栽培方法对农作物品种变化的影响。在手工业方面，书中内容涵盖了纺织业、陶瓷生产、冶炼业、机械制造业等当时主要生产行业。书中记录了诸多当时处于世界领先地位的技术成就，比如最先进的纺织机械“花机”，从生铁到熟铁再合炼成钢的生产系统，以及最先进的鼓风设备“活塞式风箱图”，等等。

该书在东亚和欧美都有着广泛的传播和影响，被誉为“中国17世纪的工艺百科全书”，曾直接推动欧洲农业革命，并帮助缓解欧洲造纸业的原料危机。该书蕴含的“天人合一”理念和人本主义科技伦理思想，对于当今人与自然、人与科技的探讨依然具有启示意义。

Tiangong Kaiwu (*The Exploitation of the Works of Nature*)

Tiangong Kaiwu was the world's first comprehensive work on agriculture and handicraft production. It was first published in 1637 by the Ming Dynasty scientist Song Yingxing (1587-c.1666). The book covers 18 fields, documents over 130 techniques and tools, and features 123 vivid illustrations.

Regarding agriculture, the book discusses the impact of soil, climate conditions, and cultivation methods on the evolvement of crop varieties. On handicraft making, the book covers the main industries of the time, such as textiles, ceramics, metallurgy, and machinery. It records many technological achievements that were world-leading at the time, such as a textile machine called "flower machine", a metalwork technique that combined pig iron, wrought iron, and steel, and an advanced air blowing device – piston bellows – among others.

Known as the "Encyclopedia of Crafts in 17th Century China", the book was widely disseminated in East Asia and Europe and had a significant impact. It was instrumental in promoting the agricultural revolution in Europe and alleviating the raw material crisis in European papermaking. The concept of "unity of heaven and man" and the humanistic ethical ideas of science and technology contained in the book still provide inspiration for today's exploration of the relationship between humanity, nature, and technology.

《营造法式》

中国古代建筑学著作《营造法式》由北宋官员李诫（1035—1110）主持编修，是北宋官方颁布的建筑设计资料集和建筑规范丛书，被誉为“中国古代建筑百科全书”。

《营造法式》成书于北宋元符三年（1100），正文共34卷，分为4个部分。第一、第二卷为《总释》《总例》，对书中的建筑和构件术语进行规范诠释；第三卷至第十五卷介绍了13个建筑工种的营造规范；第十六卷至第二十八卷规定了各工种的用工及用料的定额标准、计算方法以及质量标准；第二十九至第三十四卷是各类建筑及构件的平面图、剖面图、彩画图等图样。英国著名科技史学家李约瑟认为，这些图样在框架组合与精细程度上，远远超过西方中世纪大教

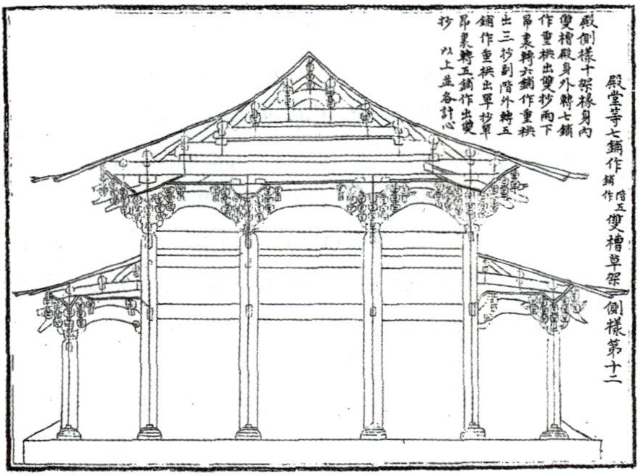

Yingzao Fashi (Standards and Models for Architecture)

Yingzao Fashi (*Standards and Models for Architecture*) is a set of books on standards and knowhows of architectures. It was compiled under the auspices of Li Jie (1035-1110), an official in the Northern Song Dynasty (960-1127), and is crowned as the encyclopedia of ancient Chinese architecture.

The revision of *Yingzao Fashi* was finished in 1100, the third year of Yuanfu period of the Emperor Zhezong's reign in the Northern Song Dynasty. The book comprises 34 volumes, which are divided into four sections. The first two volumes are *Zongshi* (The General Glossary) and *Zongli* (The General Regulations), which provide an explanation of the technical terms about constructions and components. Volume 3 to 15 introduces the construction norms regarding 13 types of construction work; volume16 to 28 are about the number of laborers and materials that should be used for each type of work, calculating methods and quality standards; volume 29 to 34 are illustrations of various constructions, including architectural plans, sections, colored plans, etc. Renowned historian of science Joseph Needham believed that these illustrations are much better than the western graphics of medieval cathedrals and the

◀《营造法式》原书插图
"Yingzao Fashi (Standards and models for architecture) "

堂的制图与阿拉伯机械图样。

《营造法式》系统总结了北宋及前代建筑设计施工的方法和经验，反映了中国古代建筑工匠的卓越才能和高超技艺，是中国古籍中最早、最完备的一部建筑技术专著，也是世界上正式印刷出版的第一部建筑学专著，对后世建筑技艺的发展具有重要影响。

Arabic mechanic graphics in terms of framework combination and accuracy.

Yingzao Fashi systematically summarizes the methods and experience concerning architecture design and construction until the Northern Song Dynasty, which epitomizes the excellent talent and outstanding skills of ancient Chinese architects and craftsmen. Being the earliest and most comprehensive book on architecture, as well as the world's first printed and published architectural monograph, *Yingzao Fashi* has profound influence on the development of architectural craftsmanship in later times.

《徐霞客游记》

中国古代地理学名著《徐霞客游记》由明代徐弘祖（1586—1641）著。徐弘祖，字振之，号霞客。《徐霞客游记》用日记体记载了作者自1613年至1639年间的旅行考察，是一部文学性强、内容丰富的旅游百科全书，更是一部重要的古代地理科学文献。

《徐霞客游记》详细记载了山川源流、地形地貌、动植矿物等内容，开启了中国地理学界系统观察自然、描写自然的新方向，是中国古代地理学面向实地考察，探索自然地理变化成因的代表作品，对中国古代地理学的科学化、系统化发展起到了重要作用，其影响至今尚存。《徐霞客游记》还详细记录了游历当地经济贸易、民风习俗、城镇村寨、民族关系、民间宗教等方面内容，文辞优美、包罗万象，对研究明清历史具有重要参考价值。

The Travel Diaries of Xu Xiake

An ancient Chinese geographic masterpiece, *The Travel Diaries of Xu Xiake* was written by Xu Hongzu (1586-1641) during the Ming Dynasty (1368-1644). Xu Hongzu, also known as Xu Xiake, recorded his travels and explorations from 1613 to 1639 in the form of a diary. The book is a literary masterpiece, a comprehensive travel encyclopedia, and an important work of ancient geographical science.

The book provides detailed records of the origins of mountains and rivers, the terrain and landforms, and flora, fauna, and minerals. It opened up a new path for observing and describing nature. A representative work of ancient Chinese geography, it focuses on field observations and explores the causes of natural geographic changes. It played an important role in the development of ancient Chinese geography and remains influential to this day. In addition, the book also includes detailed records of local trade, customs, towns and villages, ethnic relations, and folk religions. Expressed in beautiful language and covering a wide range of topics, the book has significant reference value for the study of Ming and Qing (1368-1911) history.

瓷器

中国是瓷器的故乡，多姿多彩的瓷器是中国古代的伟大发明之一，也是中华民族对世界文明的伟大贡献。中国是最先发明瓷器的国家，外国人把中国称作“瓷器之国”，英语中的“China”既名瓷器，又称中国。

瓷器由瓷石、高岭土、石英石、莫来石等烧制而成，外表施有玻璃质釉或彩绘。在高温烧制过程中，瓷器的胎料和釉色因温度不同而发生各种化学变化，形成不同的质地、色彩和纹饰，使不同时期、不同产地的瓷器精美雅致、各具特色。宋朝的白瓷、元代的青花瓷、明清的五彩瓷是中国瓷器发展史上的典型代表。江西景德镇因制瓷工艺闻名于世，

Porcelain

China, the birthplace of porcelain, boasts a rich and vibrant history of porcelain-making that represents one of the country's greatest inventions and contributions to world civilization. As the country that invented porcelain, China has long been known as the "Porcelain Kingdom" and the word "China" in English refers to both porcelain and the country itself.

Porcelain is made from materials such as porcelain stone, kaolin, feldspar, and quartz, and is coated with glass glazes or decorated with painted designs. During the high-temperature firing process, the materials and glazes undergo various chemical changes, resulting in different textures, colors, and patterns that are unique to different periods and regions. Typical examples of Chinese porcelain include the white porcelain of the Song Dynasty (960-1279), blue-and-white porcelain of the Yuan Dynasty (1271-1368), and polychrome porcelain of the Ming and Qing dynasties (1368-1911). Jingdezhen in Jiangxi Province is renowned for its porcelain-mak-

历史上曾为皇室制作瓷器长达900多年，被称为中国的“瓷都”。这些瓷器精品不仅体现了古代中国领先世界的技艺水平，更承载着东方世界的独特文化和审美。

作为来自东方的艺术品，中国瓷器是中华传统文化的重要标识，也是古代丝绸之路上的重要货物，自唐朝开始就远销海外。瓷器贸易推动了世界物质和技术交流，其蕴含的丰富人文内涵，对中外文明交流互鉴和世界文化发展产生了深远影响。

ing craftsmanship, which dates back more than 900 years and produced porcelain for the imperial court, earning the city the title of "Porcelain Capital of China". Porcelain masterpieces showcase the high-level technological expertise of ancient China, and embody the unique cultural and aesthetic values of the East.

As an art form from the East, Chinese porcelain was an important symbol of traditional Chinese culture and an important commodity along the ancient Silk Road. Porcelain trade facilitated material and technological exchanges across the world and its rich cultural meanings informed cross-cultural communication and the development of world culture.

文学

Literature

文学超越文字简单的记录功能，表达出人类丰富的思想和情感。流传至今的上古神话，成为中国浪漫主义文学的源头。从《诗经》、楚辞到汉赋、唐诗、宋词、元曲以及明清小说，一大批才华横溢的文学家陆续登场，留下了浩如烟海的文学作品。中国文学讲究“文以载道”，主张超越作家一己之悲欢，充分表达中国人的思维方式和价值观念。

Beyond the simple function of recording information in written form, literature reveals profound thoughts and emotions of humanity. Ancient myths that have been passed down to the present day serve as a source of Chinese romantic literature. An impressive number of talented writers have emerged throughout China's history, leaving behind an equally impressive number of literary works, from the "Classic of Poetry" and "Chu Ci" to Han Fu , Tang poetry, Song Ci, Yuan drama, and the Ming-Qing novel. Chinese literature emphasizes the importance of "using words to explain ideas" and encourages writers to transcend their own sorrows and joys in favor of expressing shared Chinese values.

盘古开天

盘古是中国神话里开天辟地创造人类世界的始祖，传说天地及万物都由其身躯和器官转化而成。相传很久以前，天、地没有形成，宇宙混沌一片，就像一个浑圆的鸡蛋。有个叫盘古的巨人，在这片黑暗和混沌中孕育了一万八千年。有一天，盘古突然醒来，见周围一片漆黑，就抡起大斧头劈开了混沌的世界。黑暗渐渐散开，轻而清的东西，缓缓上升，变成了天；重而浊的东西，慢慢下降，变成了地。天地分开后，盘古怕它们还会合在一起，便头顶着天，脚蹬着地，站在天地当中，随着它们的变化而变化。天每天升高一丈，地每天增厚一丈，盘古的身体也跟着长高。又过了许多年，天和地逐渐成形，盘古也精疲力竭，累得倒下了。他庞大的身躯倒在大地上，创造出一个充满生机的世界：他的呼吸变为寒暑，吹出的气息变成了四季的风和飘动的云；他发出的声音化作了隆隆的雷声；他的双眼变成了太阳和月亮，头发、胡须变成满天星辰；他的肌肤变成了辽阔的大地；他的四肢和躯干化作大地的四极和五方的名山，汗毛化为花草树木，骨骼化为金银，牙齿变成玉石；他的汗水化为滋

The Legend of Pan Gu Creating the World

Pan Gu is a pivotal figure in Chinese mythology, revered as the ancestral creator of the world and humanity. According to legend, before the formation of heaven, earth, and all things, the universe existed in a state of chaos, likened to a round egg. In this chaotic world, a giant named Pan Gu incubated in the darkness and chaos for 18,000 years. One day, he suddenly awakened and found himself surrounded by pitch-blackness. Using his massive axe, he split open the chaotic world, causing the darkness to disperse. Light and clear things gradually rose and became the sky, while heavy and turbid things sank and formed the earth.

After separating heaven and earth, Pan Gu feared that they would come back together, so he stood between them, holding up the sky with his head and standing on the earth with his feet, changing with them as they transformed. Every day, the sky rose one zhang (about 3.3 meters), the earth thickened one zhang, and Pan Gu's body grew taller. Eventually, after many years, the sky and earth took shape, and Pan Gu grew exhausted and fell to the ground.

Pan Gu's massive body lay on the ground, creating a vibrant world. His breath became cold air and heat, blowing out as the winds of the four seasons and drifting clouds. The sound he made became the thunder, and his eyes became the sun and moon. His hair and beard transformed into the stars in the sky, while his skin became the vast earth. His limbs and trunk became the four poles of the earth and great mountains. His

润万物的雨露，血液化作奔流不息的江海……从此人世间便有了阳光雨露，大地上有了江河湖海，万物滋长，人类繁衍生息。

无论东方还是西方，很多国家和民族都有自己的创世纪传说。中国神话盘古开辟天地，反映出中国古人对于宇宙形成的浪漫想象，体现出中华民族向往光明、无私奉献的精神。

hair became flowers, plants, and trees, and his bones became gold and silver while his teeth turned into precious stones. His sweat became the rain and dew that nourished all things, and his blood became flowing rivers and seas.

As a result, the world has sunshine and rain, rivers and lakes; everything grows; and humanity thrives.

Just as many countries and cultures, whether in the East or the West, have their own myths of how the world came into existence, this Chinese mythology details the ancient people's imaginative and romantic notion of how the universe was formed, while also embodying the Chinese people's yearning for enlightenment and their celebration of a selfless spirit.

夸父追日

夸父追日是出自《山海经》的古代神话。夸父是远古时期的一位巨人，住在北方荒野的一座大山上。北方夏季短暂，冬季漫长寒冷，太阳每天从东方升起，又匆匆向西边落下。夸父希望太阳永不落下，不断地给大地带来光和热，让寒冷的北方和江南一样温暖。于是他大步朝太阳落山的方向追去。当夸父追到太阳落入山谷之际已是口干舌燥，便喝干了黄河和渭河的水，却还是没有解渴，后来在去北方大湖找水的途中不幸干渴而亡。夸父临终前抛掉手里的桃木杖，木杖落地的地方顿时生出一片茂盛的桃林并结出鲜桃，为后来追求光明的路人遮阴、解渴。

夸父追日的故事，反映了中国古代人民了解自然、战胜自然的朴素愿望和顽强精神。

Kuafu Chasing the Sun

"Kuafu Chasing the Sun" is a well-known Chinese myth that originated from the *Shan Hai Jing* or the *Classic of Mountains and Seas*. The myth tells the story of Kuafu, a giant who lived on a vast mountain in the northern wilderness. In the north, the summer was brief, and the winter was long and icebound. Every day, the sun would rise in the east and swiftly set in the west. Kuafu wished to catch the sun and prevent it from setting to bring perpetual light and warmth to the land.

So Kuafu set out westwards on his quest to chase the sun. When he arrived at the valley where the sun had set, he was already exhausted and thirsty. So he drank all the water from the Yellow River and the Weihe River, but this was not enough to quench his thirst. Undeterred, he continued the chase and eventually died of thirst on his way to the northern lake.

Before he died, he discarded his peach wood staff, which miraculously sprouted into a lush peach forest. The forest provided shade and shelter for travelers, and the peaches quenched their thirst.

The story embodies the ancient Chinese desire to understand nature and the unwavering determination to conquer it.

精卫填海

精卫填海是出自《山海经》的古代神话。上古时期，炎帝教人用火烧荒，耕种田地，成为各部落共同尊奉的首领。有一天，炎帝最小的女儿女娃在东海游玩时，不幸被波涛吞没。女娃死后，她的精魂化作了一只小鸟，每天从西山上衔来石头和草木，投入东海，决心要把大海填平。她成年累月，往复飞翔，从不停息；一边填海，还一边发出“精卫、精卫”的悲鸣，好像在呼唤着从前的自己。人们便给这只鸟取名为“精卫”。

精卫鸟志在以自身微弱的力量填平大海，反映了中国古代人民锲而不舍的精神和与命运抗争到底的勇气。

Jingwei's Attempt to Fill the Sea

"Jingwei's Attempt to Fill the Sea" is an ancient Chinese myth from the *Shan Hai Jing*. In ancient times, the Yan Emperor taught people to use fire to clear wasteland and cultivate farmland, and he became the leader respected by all tribes. One day, his youngest daughter drowned while boating on the East Sea. After her death, her spirit was transformed into a small bird that carried pebbles, grass, and twigs from the western mountains and threw them into the East Sea every day, determined to fill it up. The bird worked tirelessly while making mournful cries of "Jingwei, Jingwei", as if calling out to her former self. People named this bird "Jingwei".

The story of Jingwei bird, who was determined to fill the vast ocean with her own meager strength, reflects the spirit of perseverance of the ancient Chinese and their courage to overcome adversity.

愚公移山

愚公移山是出自《列子》的古代寓言故事。相传北山山下住着一位名叫愚公的老人。他的家门南面有两座大山挡住了出路。在年已九十岁时，愚公下决心率领他的儿孙们上山，凿石挖土，想要挖走这两座大山。有个名叫智叟的老人讥笑愚公一家这样干太愚蠢了，认为仅凭愚公父子几人要挖掉这两座大山是完全不可能的。愚公回答说："我虽然老了，但我死后有我的儿子，还有孙子，子子孙孙是没有穷尽的。而这两座山却不会再增高了，挖一点就会少一点，怎么会挖不平呢?"春去秋来，愚公移山的意志不变，日夜搬山不止。愚公的坚持感动了天帝，他派两个神仙下凡，背走了那两座山，帮助愚公实现了移山通路的理想。

愚公移山的故事，反映了中国古代劳动人民的信心和毅力，体现了中华民族知难而进、艰苦奋斗的精神。千百年来，愚公移山的故事广为流传，愚公移山精神成为中华优秀传统文化的重要标识。

Yu Gong Moving Mountains

The story of "Yu Gong Moving Mountains" is a ancient fable from the book *Liezi*. According to legend, an old man named Yu Gong lived at the foot of two great mountains in the north. The mountains blocked the way for him and his family. At the age of ninety, Yu Gong decided to lead his sons and grandsons in an attempt to remove the mountains. An old man named Zhi Sou ridiculed Yu Gong and his family, saying that it was foolish to attempt to move such large mountains with only a few people. Yu Gong replied, "Although I am old and will die, I have sons and grandsons who will continue the work, and their sons and grandsons will do the same. The mountains, on the other hand, will not grow any taller, and as we dig away a little bit at a time, why shouldn't we be able to remove them?"

Spring passed and autumn arrived, but Yu Gong's determination remained unwavering. His persistence moved the Heavenly Emperor, who sent two gods down to the earth to carry the mountains away, helping Yu Gong to realize his dream of a clear path through the mountains.

The story of Yu Gong is one about confidence and perseverance of the working people of ancient China and embodies the spirit of the Chinese nation to forge ahead in the face of difficulties and strive for success through hard work. For thousands of years, this story has circulated widely, and the spirit of Yu Gong removing the mountains has become an important symbol of traditional Chinese culture.

《诗经》

《诗经》是中国最早的一部诗歌总集，是中国古代诗歌的开端。《诗经》收录了西周初年至春秋中叶（约前11世纪—前6世纪）的诗歌，共311篇。西周初年，朝廷派出专门的使者在农忙时到全国各地采集民谣，由史官和乐师编纂整理后给天子看，目的是了解民情。

按内容不同，《诗经》可分为《风》《雅》《颂》三部分。《风》又称《国风》，大多数是民间诗歌，带有浓烈的地域色彩，共160篇。《雅》是指周朝统治地区的音乐，分为宴请宾客的音乐《小雅》和群臣朝拜的音乐《大雅》，共105篇。《颂》是宗庙祭祀用的诗歌，分为《周颂》《鲁颂》和《商颂》，共40篇。

《诗经》内容丰富，真实反映了周代社会生活方方面面，其朴素自然的艺术风格、优美丰富的语言表达，对中国文学发展产生了深远影响。

The Book of Songs

The Book of Songs is China's earliest collection of poetry. It offers a window into how poetry emerged in ancient times. It contains 311 poems from the early Western Zhou Dynasty to the mid-Spring and Autumn Period (approximately from the 11th century B.C. to the 6th century B.C.). During the early Western Zhou Dynasty, the royal court dispatched envoys to collect folk songs across the land during the busy farming seasons. These songs were then compiled and edited by official historians and musicians to allow the ruler to have a glimpse of his people's lives and their opinions.

The Book of Songs can be divided into three parts based on the topics they deal with: *Airs of the States* or *guofeng*; *Hymns* or *ya*; and *Eulogies* or *song*. *Airs of the States* are mostly folk poems totaling 160 with strong regional characteristics. *Hymns* are musical pieces used in ceremonies and banquets during the Zhou Dynasty (770-256 B.C.). They are further divided into *Minor Court Hymns* and *Major Court Hymns*, totaling 105 poems. *Eulogies* are religious poems used in imperial sacrifices, including *Eulogies of Zhou*, *Eulogies of Lu*, and *Eulogies of Shang*, totaling 40 poems.

The Book of Songs reflects various aspects of life during the Zhou Dynasty. Its simple and natural artistic style, together with its beautiful, rich and expressive language, has had a profound impact on the development of Chinese literature.

《山海经》

《山海经》是一部神话地理志，成书于战国时期至汉代初期，全书现存18篇，其中《山经》5篇、《海经》9篇、《大荒经》4篇。这一古籍以山为纲，详细描述了每座山的地理位置、走向及动植物形态、矿产分布，记叙了河流发源、流向以及主要水系和支流的分布情况。

《山海经》还记录了上古时期人们的生活状况和思想活动，涵盖上古地理、历史、神话、天文、动物、植物、医学、宗教、人类学、民族学、海洋学、科技史等方面内容，勾勒出了上古时期的文明与文化状态，被视为上古社会生活的百科全书。此外，《山海经》保存了大量的上古神话传说、巫术信仰和种种奇思妙想，如夸父追日、女娲补天、精卫填海、后羿射日、大禹治水、黄帝战蚩尤等故事，寄托了华夏先民奇幻瑰丽的想象，成为后世文学家、艺术家的灵感宝库。

Shan Hai Jing (*Classic of Mountains and Seas*)

Shan Hai Jing, a mythological and geographical text, was compiled from the Warring States period (475-221 B.C.) to the early Han Dynasty (206 B.C.-A.D. 220). The extant text consists of 18 chapters, including five on mountains, nine on seas, and four on the wilderness. The book focuses on mountains, and provides detailed descriptions of their location and orientation as well as their flora and fauna and the distribution of minerals. It also documents the sources, flows, and distributions of major water systems and their tributaries.

Shan Hai Jing also records the living conditions and intellectual pursuits of ancient people, covering a wide range of subjects such as geography, history, mythology, astronomy, flora and fauna, medicine, religion, anthropology, ethnology, oceanography, and the history of science and technology. It outlines the civilization and culture of the ancient period and is regarded as an encyclopedia of ancient society. It also contains numerous ancient myths, witchcraft beliefs, and imaginative ideas, such as the stories of Kuafu chasing the sun, Nvwa mending the sky, Jingwei filling the sea, Houyi shooting the suns, Yu controlling the floods, and Huangdi fighting Chiyou. These stories embody the fantastic imagination of the ancient Chinese, and have been a source of inspiration for writers and artists of later periods.

陶渊明

陶渊明（约365—427），东晋南北朝时期著名诗人。陶渊明出身仕宦之家，却一心务农隐居，是隐逸诗人的代表。

陶渊明在思想上坚守儒家伦理，又爱好道家自由。他是中国田园诗的开创者，作品往往以隐逸生活和人生苦短为主题，所写田园风景闲静和穆、超尘脱俗，几乎“篇篇有酒”。他的诗歌绝大部分是五言诗，风格平和淡远，代表作有《归园田居》《饮酒》等。他的散文代表作是《桃花源记》，描写了在恬静的田园中，男女老幼生活安宁富足，他们亲切善良，长期与外界隔绝，对世事变迁一无所知，生活在自由自在的状态中。后来，桃花源成为中国式乌托邦的象征。

Tao Yuanming

Tao Yuanming (c. 365-427) was a renowned poet of the Eastern Jin and Northern and Southern dynasties (317-589). Despite being born into a family of officials, he devoted himself to farming and seclusion and became a leading figure among reclusive poets.

Tao adhered to Confucian ethics in his thoughts, but also had a fondness for the freedom of Taoism. He was the founder of Chinese pastoral poetry, and his works often focus on the themes of seclusion and the brevity of life, depicting pastoral scenery as tranquil, pure, and detached from worldly affairs, with almost every one of his works mentioning wine. Most of his poetry is in the form of five-character verses, characterized by a gentle and distant style. His representative works include *Returning to the Fields and Gardens* and *Drinking Wine*. His best-known prose work is *The Peach Blossom Spring*, which describes the peaceful and prosperous life of men and women, old and young, in a quiet pastoral area. They are kind and friendly to each other, and having been isolated from the outside world for a long time, they live in a state of freedom and ease. Later, *The Peach Blossom Spring* became a symbol of Chinese utopia.

李白

李白（701—762），唐代伟大的浪漫主义诗人。李白为人爽朗大方，乐于交友，爱好饮酒作诗，想象奇特丰富，气势豪迈奔放，人称“诗仙”。

李白著有《李太白集》，代表作有《静夜思》《赠汪伦》《将进酒》《望庐山瀑布》等。他的诗中常综合运用想象、夸张、比喻、拟人等手法，从而营造出瑰丽动人的意境，展现了浪漫主义诗作风格，对后世诗人产生了深远影响。

Li Bai

Li Bai (701-762) was a great romantic poet of the Tang Dynasty (618-907). Known as the "Poet Immortal", he was a generous and outgoing person who enjoyed making friends, drinking, and creating poetry. Li Bai was known for his unique and abundant imagination, as well as his grand and unrestrained style of poetry.

Li Bai's representative works are collected in *The Collected Works of Li Taibai*, which includes *Quiet Night Thoughts*, *To Wang Lun*, *Taking Wine*, *Looking at the Waterfall on Mount Lu* among others. In his poetry, Li Bai often employs imagination, exaggeration, metaphor and personification, creating beautiful and moving imagery and showcasing the style of romanticism in poetry, which had a profound influence on poets in later periods.

杜甫

杜甫（712—770），唐代伟大的现实主义诗人。杜甫的诗以宏大的社会写实著称，深刻反映了唐代安史之乱前后20多年的社会面貌，被称为“诗史”。杜甫的诗中蕴含儒家思想，洋溢着仁民爱物的情怀和爱国主义色彩，因而他被尊为“诗圣”。

杜甫一生颠沛流离，他善用理智去仔细观察人生社会的实况，用自己的生活经验去体察人民的苦乐，具有强烈的政治意识。他的诗以浑朴沉郁的风格著称，代表作有《登高》《春望》《北征》《茅屋为秋风所破歌》等，对中国文学和日本文学都产生了深远的影响。

Du Fu

Du Fu (712-770) was a great realistic poet of the Tang Dynasty (618-907). His poems are known for their broad social realism, and provide a profound reflection on society in the two decades before and after the An Lushan Rebellion. They are referred to as "poetic history". His poetry reflects Confucianism, and is full of the compassionate love of the people, affection for all living things, and a patriotic spirit, making him a revered "Poet Saint".

Du lived a life of constant turmoil and displacement. He observed the realities of life and society with a keen sense of reason and empathy, drawing from his own experiences to empathize with the joys and sorrows of the people, and demonstrating a strong political consciousness. His poetry is known for its simple and melancholic style, as reflected in works such as *Ascending the Heights*, *Spring Prospect*, *Northern Expedition*, and *My Cottage Unroofed by Autumn Gales*. His influence on both Chinese and Japanese literature is profound.

苏轼

苏轼（1037—1101），宋代著名文学家，宋代文学最高成就的代表。苏轼的诗歌题材丰富、风格旷达，他首创词坛“豪放”一派，是中国文化史上罕见的通才、全才，在散文、诗词、绘画领域都有着极高的造诣。其代表作有《赤壁赋》《水调歌头·明月几时有》等。苏轼还是一位美食家，创造出“东坡肉”等饮食精品。

苏轼出身平民之家，青年时期就确立了为民请命的民本情怀，将“民为天下之本”作为一生笃行的从政理念。他因直言敢谏而屡受排挤，宦海沉浮，多次被贬。尽管身处逆境，苏轼却保持超然态度，随遇而安，始终坚守为国为民的初心，深受百姓爱戴。苏轼这种历经沧桑而初心不改、饱经风霜而本色依旧的精神为后世景仰，成为中华文化推崇的宝贵品质。

Su Shi

Su Shi (1037-1101), also known as Su Dongpo, was a renowned literary figure during the Song Dynasty (960-1279) and the icon of the highest achievements in Song Dynasty literature. His poetry was characterized by rich themes and an expansive style. He was the founder of the "bold" style in the *ci* poetry form, and was a rare polymath in China's cultural history, achieving great successes in prose, poetry, and painting. His representative works include *My Visit to the Red Cliffs* and *Prelude to Water Melody*. Su Shi was also a gourmet and created culinary masterpieces such as "Dongpo Pork".

Su Shi came from a humble family, but in his youth he developed a strong sense of serving the people, and made "the people are the foundation of the world" his lifelong political philosophy. Due to his outspokenness and readiness to offer advice, he was often marginalized and exiled. Despite numerous setbacks, Su Shi maintained a detached attitude, adapting to his circumstances, and remained true to his original aspiration of serving the country and the people. His devotion to the people earned him their deep love and respect. His unwavering commitment to his beliefs in the face of adversity has been admired by later generations, making it a cherished trait in Chinese culture.

李清照

李清照（1084—1155），北宋著名女词人，婉约派代表，有“千古第一才女”之称。李清照出身书香门第，儿时在良好的家庭环境中打下扎实的文学基础。她婚后与丈夫赵明诚共同致力于书画金石的搜集整理，生活美满。这一时期，她的作品热情活泼，明快天真，多写无忧无虑的少女生活、婚后对丈夫的离别相思等，充分表现了闺阁女性的丰富感情。后来，在因战乱流落南方后，她因丈夫去世、国破家亡而颠沛流离、孤独无依，在词作中多表现为缠绵凄苦，深沉伤感。

李清照的词既有婉约温馨，又有刚强健举，还有高远飞扬，突破了传统女性词作的风格桎梏，成为中国古代文学史上独立自主的女性诗词人代表。

Li Qingzhao

Li Qingzhao (1084-1155) was a renowned female *ci* poet of the Northern Song Dynasty (960-1127), known for her delicate style. She was widely regarded as the "preeminent female talent of all time". Born into a scholarly family, Li was given a solid literary foundation during her childhood. After marrying Zhao Mingcheng, she led a happy life and devoted herself to the collection and arrangement of calligraphy, painting, and inscriptions. During this period her works were lively and optimistic, often depicting carefree girlhood and the longing for her husband after they were separated. Her writings fully expressed the rich emotions of women in the boudoir. Later, due to war and turmoil, she was forced to flee to the south. After her husband's death and the fall of her homeland, Li Qingzhao's life was filled with hardship and loneliness. Her works turned melancholic and poignant, reflecting her deep emotions and the sorrows of her time.

Li's poetry exhibits a unique blend of delicacy and strength, tenderness and determination, and lofty aspirations that transcend the traditional constraints imposed upon female poets. She stood out as an exemplar of independent and self-assured female poets in ancient Chinese literature.

《三国演义》

《三国演义》是中国古典小说四大名著之一，也是中国文学史上第一部长篇章回体历史演义小说，作者是元末明初的罗贯中（约1330—约1400）。《三国演义》描写的是从东汉末年到西晋初年近百年间群雄割据的历史，叙写了魏、蜀、吴三国之间的政治和军事斗争，反映了三国时期各类社会斗争和矛盾的转化。它大致根据史书《三国志》的记载，将三国历史中的忠奸是非，以通俗易懂的方式进行解说。

《三国演义》刻画了400多个人物形象，脍炙人口的人物包括诸葛亮（181—234）、曹操（155—220）、关羽（？—219）、刘备（161—223）等。书中描绘的诸葛亮是贤臣的化身，曹操是有野心和才智的奸雄，关羽是义重如山的名将，刘备则是仁君典型。

在中国人心中，小说《三国演义》的巨大影响力甚至

Romance of the Three Kingdoms

Romance of the Three Kingdoms is widely regarded as one of the Four Great Classics of Chinese literature, and is considered to be the first historical novel written in the form of a lengthy episodic narrative. Written by Luo Guanzhong (c. 1330–c. 1400), the novel tells the story of the political and military struggles among the states of Wei, Shu, and Wu during the turbulent period from the end of the Eastern Han Dynasty (25-220) to the beginning of the Western Jin Dynasty (265-317), spanning almost a hundred years. Based on the *Records of the Three Kingdoms*, the novel vividly reflects the complex social struggles and conflicts that occurred during the Three Kingdoms period, and presents the concepts of loyalty and treachery in a way that is both easy to understand and deeply insightful.

The novel portrays over 400 characters, including some of the most iconic figures in Chinese literature. These include Zhuge Liang (181-234), Cao Cao (155-220), Guan Yu (?-219), and Liu Bei (161-223). Zhuge Liang is depicted as the embodiment of wisdom and virtue, while Cao Cao is portrayed as an ambitious and intelligent villain whose actions are driven by his desire for power. Guan Yu is celebrated as a legendary general who values loyalty and righteousness above all else, and Liu Bei is presented as a model ruler who embodies benevolence and virtue.

In Chinese culture, *Romance of the Three Kingdoms* is seen as an incredibly influential novel, with its impact even sur-

盖过了真实历史，取材于它的文艺作品不胜枚举。《三国演义》还先后被译成数十种文字，在世界上许多国家广泛流传，尤其受到亚洲各国人民的喜爱。

passing that of the actual historical events it portrays. Countless works of literature and art have drawn inspiration from the novel. It has also been translated into dozens of languages and widely circulated across the globe, with a particularly strong following in various other Asian countries.

《西游记》

《西游记》是中国古典小说四大名著之一，也是中国古代第一部长篇神魔小说，富有浪漫主义色彩。《西游记》成书于16世纪明朝中叶，作者是吴承恩（约1500—约1582）。

《西游记》在宋、元以来关于玄奘取经的故事和有关作品基础上创作而成。书中主要讲述了唐三藏与孙悟空、猪八戒和沙和尚师徒四人前往西天取经，一路上历经艰险，降妖除魔，经历了九九八十一难，终于见到如来佛祖，取回真经、修成正果的故事。

《西游记》系统地反映了中国儒、释、道三教合流的思想体系，将道教的天宫、地狱和海洋的神仙体系与佛教的西天糅合到一起，并借神魔故事批判现实世界，歌颂了孙悟空自由勇敢的精神，表现了惩恶扬善的古老主题。书中孙悟

Journey to the West

The novel *Journey to the West* is one of the Four Great Classics. It is also recognized as the first epic-length novel in ancient Chinese literature that features gods, demons, and a strong element of romanticism. The novel was written by Wu Cheng'en (c. 1500-c. 1582) in the mid-16th century during the Ming Dynasty (1368-1644).

It is a literary work that draws upon the story of Xuanzang's pilgrimage to get Buddhist scriptures, as well as earlier works from the Song and Yuan dynasties (960-1368). The book tells the epic tale of Tang Sanzang, a Buddhist monk, and his three disciples: Sun Wukong (The Monkey King), Zhu Bajie (Piggy), and Sha Wujing (Sandy), as they embark on a perilous journey to the west. Along the way they face a series of challenges, battle demons and monsters, and endure eighty-one tribulations. Their ultimate goal is to meet the Buddha and be given the sacred scriptures, which they achieve after much hardship and struggle.

Journey to the West reflects the ideological convergence of Confucianism, Buddhism, and Taoism in China. It blends the celestial beings of Taoism's heavenly palace, underworld, and ocean with Buddhism's Western Paradise, and critiques the real world through the stories of gods and monsters, while praising the bravery and free spirit of Sun Wukong. The book also expresses the ancient theme of promoting good and punishing evil. The characters of Sun Wukong, Tang Sanzang, Zhu Bajie, and Sha Wujing, as well as the stories of "The Monkey King

空、唐三藏、猪八戒、沙和尚等人物形象，“大闹天宫”“三打白骨精”“三借芭蕉扇”等故事家喻户晓。几百年来，《西游记》被改编成地方戏曲、电影、电视剧、动画片、漫画等各类作品，在世界许多国家和地区广泛流传。

Wreaks Havoc in Heaven", "The Three Battles with the White-Boned Demon", and "The Three Borrowings of the Palm-Leaf Fan" are well-known to readers. For centuries, *Journey to the West* has been adapted into various works such as local operas, movies, TV series, animated films, and comics that have been widely circulated in many countries and regions around the world.

《水浒传》

《水浒传》是中国古典小说四大名著之一，也是中国历史上最早用白话文写成的长篇章回体小说之一。《水浒传》成书于元末明初，由施耐庵（1296—1370）著，罗贯中整理。小说讲述了北宋后期，山东梁山泊以宋江为首的一百零八名好汉，不满贪官污吏，爱打抱不平，先后被逼上梁山，与腐化的朝廷抗争，最后接受招安的全过程。

《水浒传》的精彩之处在于人物刻画和市井生活的描写。小说故事豪放粗犷、情节曲折复杂，人物众多、形象生动、个性鲜明、对话传神，成功塑造了宋江、林冲、李逵、鲁智深、武松等鲜明的人物形象，深刻反映了北宋年间广阔的社会生活。《水浒传》和《三国演义》奠定了中国古代长篇小说的民族风格，塑造了中华民族特有的审美心理和鉴赏习惯。

Outlaws of the Marsh

Outlaws of the Marsh is one of the Four Great Classics of Chinese literature, and one of the earliest long episodic novels written in vernacular Chinese. It was written by Shi Nai'an (1296–1370) during the late Yuan (1279-1368) and early Ming (1368-1644) dynasties, with later editing by Luo Guanzhong. The novel tells the story of 108 outlaws, led by Song Jiang, who gather at Mount Liang in the later years of the Northern Song Dynasty (960-1127). Dissatisfied with the corruption of government officials they become rebels, fighting against the government until they are eventually granted amnesty.

The brilliance of *Outlaws of the Marsh* lies in its vivid portrayal of characters and its depiction of the lives of common people. The novel balances a bold and rough style with intricate and complex plotlines, a plethora of lively characters with distinct personalities, and expressive dialogue. The book succeeds in creating distinct characters such as Song Jiang, Lin Chong, Li Kui, Lu Zhishen, and Wu Song, and provides a profound reflection of the society during the Northern Song period. *Outlaws of the Marsh* and *Romance of the Three Kingdoms* laid the foundations for the style of ancient Chinese long novels, and shaped the unique aesthetic psychology and appreciation habits of the Chinese people.

《红楼梦》

《红楼梦》是中国古典小说四大名著之一、中国古典章回体小说的巅峰之作，也是四大名著中唯一不取材自历史事件的古典小说。《红楼梦》大约成书于18世纪前期，全书共120回，一般认为前80回作者是曹雪芹（1715—1763），后40回为无名氏补写。故事主线为贾宝玉、林黛玉、薛宝钗三人的爱情悲剧，以及贾、王、史、薛四大家族的兴衰。故事从女娲补天时剩下的一块石头讲起，因此又名《石头记》。

《红楼梦》全书塑造了700多个人物形象，主要以贾宝玉及其周围的几十名女性为中心，创造了两个对比鲜明的世界：大观园的理想世界，是贾宝玉和诸姊妹的干净乐土，女子们在里面无忧无虑，永远保持青春和纯洁；大观园外的世界是肮脏堕落的，它不断摧残理想世界，直至它完全毁灭。

《红楼梦》情节丰富，布局严密，以深刻的思想底蕴和出色的艺术成就著称于世，使学术界产生了一门专门研究它的学问，即“红学”。

A Dream of Red Mansions

A Dream of Red Mansions is recognized as one of the Four Great Classical Novels and the apogee of the chapter-novel form. Unlike the other three works in the Four Great Classical Novels, it is not based on historical events. The novel was likely written in the early 18th century, and consists of 120 chapters. Cao Xueqin (1715-1763) is generally credited as the author of the first 80 chapters, with the remaining 40 chapters completed by an anonymous writer. The story centers around the tragic love triangle between Jia Baoyu, Lin Daiyu, and Xue Baochai, and the rise and fall of four great families: Jia, Wang, Shi, and Xue. The novel begins with a stone left over when the goddess Nvwa repaired the heavens. Therefore, it is also known as *The Story of the Stone*.

A Dream of Red Mansions presents more than 700 characters, with a central focus on Jia Baoyu and the dozens of women surrounding him. The novel creates two vividly contrasting worlds. One is the Grand View Garden, an ideal world that serves as a clean paradise for Jia Baoyu and his sisters. This is a place where women lead carefree lives, maintaining their youth and purity forever. In contrast, the outside world is portrayed as a corrupt and depraved place, continuously threatening the ideal world until it is ultimately destroyed.

A Dream of Red Mansions is renowned for its intricate plot and meticulous structure, as well as its profound philosophical themes and impressive artistic achievement. This has led to the establishment of a specialized field of study known as "Hongxue," or "Redology" in academic circles.

《格萨尔》

《格萨尔》始于中国西藏地区的部落时代，至今已流传1000多年。在传播过程中，说唱艺人不断丰富其内容，至今还在更新。因此，《格萨尔》以长达60万诗行成为世界上最长的史诗，同时也是世界上唯一的活态史诗，被誉为“东方荷马史诗”。

《格萨尔》讲述了西藏东部岭国国王格萨尔的降生、征战和返回天界的故事：很久以前，藏区分裂成无数小国，征战不休，苦难深重。格萨尔王降临人间，率领岭国部队降妖除魔，使百姓过上了安宁日子。后来在80岁时，格萨尔王救出身陷地狱的妻子和母亲，回到天上。

《格萨尔》运用诗歌和散文、吟唱和道白相结合的方式，将现实生活中的故事、神话、诗歌、寓言、谚语、格言等融为一体，代表着古代藏族文化的最高成就，是研究古代藏族社会历史的一部百科全书。2009年，“格萨尔史诗传统”入选联合国教科文组织人类非物质文化遗产代表作名录。

The Epic of King Gesar

The Epic of King Gesar originated in the tribal era of Tibet in China and has been passed down for over a thousand years. As it was transmitted, its oral performers constantly enriched its content, and it continues to be updated to this day. As a result, *The Epic of King Gesar* has become the world's longest epic poem, spanning 600,000 lines, and it is also the world's only living epic poem, hailed as the "The Iliad of the East."

The Epic of King Gesar is a legendary tale that recounts the birth, military campaigns, and return to heaven of King Gesar of Ling, in the eastern part of Tibet. Many years ago, the Tibetan region was divided into numerous small kingdoms, struggling and constantly at war with each other. King Gesar was born into this world and led his army to conquer demons and evil spirits, bringing peace and prosperity to the people. Later, at the age of 80, King Gesar rescued his wife and mother from hell and returned to heaven.

It combines poetry and prose, and singing and recitation, weaving together stories, myths, poems, fables, proverbs, and maxims from real life. It represents the highest achievement of ancient Tibetan culture and serves as an encyclopedia for studying the history of ancient Tibetan society. In 2009, the "Gesar Epic Tradition" was listed in the UNESCO Representative List of the Intangible Cultural Heritage of Humanity.

《江格尔》

《江格尔》是蒙古族卫拉特部的史诗，诞生于明朝时期的西域。史诗主要讲述了江格尔汗率领12位英雄、32位虎将、6000多名勇士征战四方，降伏妖魔，建立宝木巴理想国的故事。宝木巴气候舒适宜人，社会财富均衡，没有衰败，没有死亡，这体现了蒙古族人民对共同富裕的理想社会的追求。

《江格尔》结构颇为独特，没有一个贯穿始终的主角和主情节线索。数十部作品独立成篇，合成整体。其故事发生在阿尔泰山、白头山、额尔齐斯河等地，所用语言是土尔扈特蒙古语，夹杂着维吾尔、哈萨克、布鲁特等西域族群的词汇，体现了古代西域各民族语言文化的交流融通。《江格尔》是蒙古文学的最高成就，对于研究早期蒙古族的哲学思想、宗教信仰、风俗习惯等具有重要史学价值。

Jangar

Jangar is an epic poem of the Mongolian Oirat tribe, originating from the Western Regions during the Ming Dynasty (1368-1644). The epic mainly tells the story of how Jangar Khan led 12 heroes, 32 tiger generals, and more than 6,000 warriors to conquer and subdue demons and establish the ideal state of Bomba. Bomba enjoys a comfortable and pleasant climate, and balanced social wealth without decline or death, reflecting the Mongolian people's pursuit of an ideal society of common prosperity.

The structure of *Jangar* is quite unique, without a main character or a central plotline that runs throughout. Dozens of independent works form a cohesive whole. The story takes place in various locations, such as the Altai Mountains, the Baitou Mountains, and the Ertix River. The language used is Tuul Mongolian, with vocabulary borrowed from other West Asian ethnic groups such as the Uygurs, Kazakhs, and Buruts, reflecting the cultural exchange and integration among ancient West Asian communities. "Jangar" is the highest achievement of Mongolian literature, and has significant historical value for studying the philosophical thinking, religious beliefs, and customs of early Mongolian society.

《玛纳斯》

《玛纳斯》是柯尔克孜人的英雄史诗，也是全世界第二长的史诗，共有23.4万多行，仅次于《格萨尔》，被列入人类非物质文化遗产代表作名录。

《玛纳斯》产生于9至10世纪，叙述了柯尔克孜传说中的英雄玛纳斯及其子孙，前后八代人领导族人反抗异族的掠夺与奴役，争取独立自由的故事。全诗由八部组成，分别以每部主人公的名字命名，并以玛纳斯作为总名。千百年来，《玛纳斯》一直口耳相传，其演唱已经融入柯尔克孜人的生产生活，有柯尔克孜人的地方就有《玛纳斯》的演唱。

《玛纳斯》集柯尔克孜民间文学、音乐为一体，是一部珍贵的文学典籍；同时，它也是柯尔克孜民间文化的百科全书，对研究古代新疆各民族的分布和柯尔克孜历史、文化、文学、民俗等具有重要价值。

Manas

Manas is an epic of the Kirgiz people and is the second-longest epic in the world, with over 234,000 lines, second only to *The Epic of Gesar*. It is included in the Representative List of the Intangible Cultural Heritage of Humanity by UNESCO.

Manas originated in the 9th to 10th centuries and tells the story of the legendary hero Manas and his descendants, who led their people in a struggle for independence and freedom against raiding and enslavement by foreign forces. The poem consists of eight parts, each named after the hero of that section, with Manas serving as the overall title. For centuries, the epic has been passed down through oral tradition and has become an integral part of the Kirgiz people's cultural heritage. The recitation of Manas has been incorporated into the daily life of the Kirgiz people, and wherever the Kirgiz live, the epic of Manas is performed.

Manas is a valuable literary masterpiece that combines Kirgiz folk literature and music. It is also considered an encyclopedia of Kirgiz folk culture, and provides important insights into the distribution of various ethnic groups in ancient Xinjiang, as well as Kirgiz history, culture, literature, and folklore.

艺术

Art

中国传统艺术门类丰富，包括书法、绘画、音乐、戏曲、舞蹈等。那些闻名于世的艺术大家，是中华传统文化最重要的传承者和发展者；那些精彩绝伦的艺术作品，是对中华文化理念、智慧、气度和神韵最直观的体现，反映了历代中国人对美好生活的向往。中国传统艺术不仅为中华民族提供了丰厚滋养，而且为世界文明贡献了华彩篇章，至今仍然具有旺盛的生命力。

China boasts a wide variety of traditional art forms, including calligraphy, painting, music, drama, dance, and more. Renowned artists in these fields are essential to the preservation and development of traditional Chinese culture. Their masterpieces are the most direct expression of Chinese cultural concepts, wisdom, temperament, and appeal, reflecting the people's pursuit of a better life throughout history. Traditional Chinese art is a source of cultural nourishment for the Chinese nation, and has also made a significant contribution to global civilization. It continues to thrive and display great vitality even today.

甲骨文

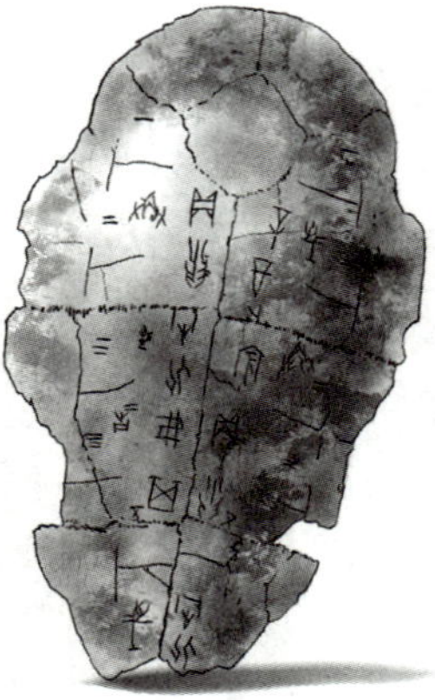

甲骨文是商朝晚期出现的中国最早的成熟文字系统，是汉字的源头和中华优秀传统文化的根脉，用以求神问卜，得知吉凶祸福。目前河南安阳小屯村的殷墟遗址是甲骨文最大的发掘地。殷墟出土的甲骨文，证实了古史记载中商王朝的存在，将中国有文字记载的历史的上限提早了约一千年。

2017年11月24日，甲骨文顺利通过联合国教科文组织世界记忆工程国际咨询委员会的评审，成功入选世界记忆名录。如今，甲骨学已成为一门蔚为壮观的世界性学科，其文字学研究对促进人类文明进步具有重要意义。

Oracle Bone Script

Oracle bone script, which emerged in the late Shang Dynasty (1600-1046 B.C.), is the earliest mature writing system in China. The source of Chinese characters and the foundation of China's excellent traditional culture, it was used for divination to inquire about good and bad luck. Currently, the Yin ruins in Xiaotun Village, Anyang, Henan Province, is the largest excavation site for oracle bone script. The oracle bone inscriptions unearthed from the Yin ruins provide important evidence of the existence of the Shang Dynasty as recorded in ancient history. This archaeological discovery has significantly extended the recorded history of China, pushing it back by approximately a millennium.

On Nov. 24, 2017, after an evaluation by the International Advisory Committee of the UNESCO Memory of the World Programme, oracle bone script was added to the UNESCO *Memory of the World Register*. Today, the study of oracle bone script has developed into a global discipline which is of great importance in promoting human civilization and progress.

篆刻

篆刻是书法和镌刻结合来制作印章的一种中国的传统艺术形式，至今已有3000多年的历史。秦汉时期，玺印成为权力和身份的象征，相传秦代丞相李斯（? 一前208）曾奉秦始皇之命，用和氏璧镌刻传国玉玺，作为中国历代正统皇帝的凭证。后来，篆刻的发展逐渐大众化，被更广泛地用作署名和收藏。时至今日，篆刻依旧流行，如2008年北京奥运会会徽就是一枚古香古色的印章图案。

篆刻是工匠精神与中华古典美学的结合，它将刀和笔结合，将汉字的千姿百态在方寸之间展现得淋漓尽致。篆刻以磅礴大气的书法、赏心悦目的构图、流畅细腻的雕刻，传递出传统艺术的独特韵味，不仅是中华民族的文化瑰宝，也是世界非物质文化遗产中的璀璨明珠。

1 2

Seal Carving

Seal carving, with a history dating back more than 3,000 years, is a traditional Chinese art form that combines calligraphy and engraving to create seals. During the Qin and Han dynasties (221 B.C.-A.D. 220), imperial seals became symbols of power and identity. Legend has it that during the Qin Dynasty, Prime Minister Li Si (?-208 B.C.) was commissioned by Emperor Qin Shi Huang to engrave the He Shi Bi jade seal, which served as proof of legitimacy for all subsequent emperors in Chinese history. Later on, seal carving gradually became more popular and was used more widely for signatures and collections. Today, seal carving is still popular, as seen in the seal emblem of the 2008 Beijing Olympic Games, which features an antique-style design.

Seal carving is a traditional art form in China that combines the spirit of craftsmanship with classical Chinese aesthetics. By the application of knife and pen, it showcases the diversity and intricacy of Chinese characters within a small space. Through grand calligraphy, pleasing composition, and smooth and delicate carving, seal carving conveys the unique charm of traditional art. It is not only a cultural treasure of the Chinese nation, but also a brilliant gem in the world's intangible cultural heritage.

◀田黄石乾隆帝三联印
The Qianlong Emperor's Three-connected Seals

1 惟精惟一 "Weijingweiyi", meaning "be pure, be of one [mind]"
2 乐天 "Letian", meaning people should be guided by heaven

文房四宝

笔、墨、纸、砚被中国文人誉为“文房四宝”。“文房四宝”是独具中国特色的文书工具，也是非物质文化遗产中极具代表性的中国国粹。

“笔”特指毛笔，笔头用动物的毛制成，最有名的是浙江湖州的“湖笔”。“墨”是书写、绘画的色料（本义是黑色，后泛指颜料），最有名的是安徽徽州所产的“徽墨”。“纸”是书写的材料，以安徽宣城生产的“宣纸”为最佳。“砚”是和水磨墨之石，最著名的是广东肇庆的“端砚”。在古代文人眼中，精美的文房用品不只是实用的工具，更是精神上的良伴。

Four Treasures of the Study

The brush, ink, paper, and inkstone, collectively known as the "Four Treasures of the Study," are highly regarded by Chinese literati as essential tools for writing and painting. These cultural artifacts are not only unique to Chinese culture but are also considered representative of China's intangible cultural heritage.

The brush, made from animal hair, is most famously produced in Huzhou, Zhejiang Province, known as the "Huzhou Brush." High quality ink, a coloring material used for writing and painting, originally black but now available in various pigments, is most famously produced in Huizhou, Anhui Province. The best paper for writing is made in Xuanzhou, Anhui Province, and known as "Xuan Paper". The inkstone, used for grinding ink with water, is most famously produced in Zhaoqing, Guangdong Province, and is known as "Duan Inkstone". In ancient times, scholars regarded these exquisite study tools not only as practical necessities but also as spiritual companions.

作为中华文明的见证者与记录者，“文房四宝”的诞生使中国迈入用其记录历史、抒发情感的时代，创造了独特风格的书法和绘画，形成了独树一帜的东方表达系统。

The emergence of the Four Treasures of the Study ushered China into an era where people could use them to record history and express their feelings. They have borne witness to and documented the development of the Chinese civilization. With these tools, Chinese people created unique styles of calligraphy and painting, establishing an distinctive expression system in this Oriental country.

王羲之

东晋书法家王羲之（303—361），是中国历史上唯一被冠以“书圣”的书法家，《兰亭集序》是其最著名的代表作，被后人称为“天下第一行书”，为世代书法家所景仰。

王羲之的书法平和自然，笔势委婉含蓄，遒美健秀，用笔细腻、结构多变，兼擅隶、草、楷、行各体，并能博采众长、融会贯通，摆脱了汉魏笔风，自成一家，创造了一代书法新风格，成为中国历代书法家临摹范本。在唐代，王羲之的书法传播到海外，对日本、韩国等国的书法艺术发展影响深远。

Wang Xizhi

Wang Xizhi (303-361), who lived in the Eastern Jin Dynasty (317-420), was the only calligrapher in Chinese history to be honored with the title of "Sage of Calligraphy". His most famous masterpiece was the *Preface to the Orchid Pavilion Collection*, which has been hailed as one of the world's finest pieces of running style calligraphy and is highly revered by generations of calligraphers.

Wang's calligraphy style is characterized by its gentle and natural flow, with brushstrokes that are elegant and subtle yet structurally varied. He was adept in various scripts, including clerical, cursive, regular, and running, and was able to draw inspiration from others to create a new style of calligraphy that departed from that of the Han and Wei dynasties. Wang's calligraphic legacy also extended beyond China, as his works were introduced to countries such as Japan and Korea during the Tang Dynasty (618-907) and exerted a profound influence on the development of calligraphy in these regions.

颜真卿

唐代著名书法家颜真卿（709—784），书法精妙，擅长行、楷。他的行书气势遒劲，正楷端庄雄伟，所创“颜体”楷书，对后世影响很大。颜真卿与欧阳询（557—641）、柳公权（778—865）、赵孟頫（1254—1322）并称为“楷书四大家”。

颜真卿的书法展现了卓越的灵性、坚强的魂魄和丰富的人生履历，故而境界瑰丽、笔力雄健、风格开阔，其传世作品以碑刻居多，代表作有《颜氏家庙碑》。颜真卿被誉为“唐朝新书体的创造者”，对于中国书法艺术的规范化具有极重要的作用，深受后世书法学习者的喜爱。

Yan Zhenqing

Yan Zhenqing (709-784) was a celebrated calligrapher in the Tang Dynasty (618-907), known for his exquisite calligraphy in both running and regular scripts. His running script is vigorous and powerful, while his regular script is dignified and grand. He created the Yan style of regular script, which exerted considerable influence on later generations. Yan Zhenqing, Ouyang Xun (557—641), Liu Gongquan (778—865), and Zhao Mengfu (1254—1322), were collectively known as the Four Masters of Regular Script.

Yan's broad range of expressions, vigorous brush strokes, and grand style demonstrated his remarkable talent, exceptional spiritual depth, and diverse life experience. His most renowned works are in the form of stone inscriptions, with the *Yan Family Temple Stele* being a notable example. Yan is known as the founder of the new Tang calligraphy style, and he played a crucial role in standardizing the art of Chinese calligraphy. He is highly revered by later generations of calligraphy practioners.

《清明上河图》

《清明上河图》是中国古典现实主义绘画的杰作，由北宋宫廷画家张择端作画，描绘了北宋宣和年间（1119—1125）都城的繁华景象。宋朝是中国艺术文化的高峰时期，思想家、诗人、画家人才辈出。北宋都城汴京（今河南省开封市）是当时世界上最大、最富裕的都城，人口100多万。《清明上河图》就把12世纪北宋全盛时期的城市面貌和人民生活状况浓缩在一幅528厘米长的画作中，流传至今。

《清明上河图》以汴河为构图中心，分三个部分展示了市郊景色、水陆交通枢纽周边和市区街市的景象。作者以长卷形式，采用“散点透视法”组织画面，如实且精细地描绘了绅士、官吏、仆役、贩夫、车轿夫、作坊工人、说书艺人、理发匠、医生、妇女、僧人、儿童、乞丐等各类人物500余人，家畜、房屋、城楼、桥梁、船只、车辆、轿子等日常街市生活元素各有特色，画卷中各类人物、景物、货物细节井然有序，画面长而不冗、繁而不乱，严密紧凑又富有

Along the River During the Qingming Festival

Along the River During the Qingming Festival is a masterpiece of classical painting in China, renowned for its realistic style. Painted by Zhang Zeduan, a court painter of the Northern Song Dynasty (960-1127), it vividly captures the bustle of daily life in the capital during the Xuanhe period (1119-1125) of the Northern Song Dynasty. The Song Dynasty (960-1279) represented a pinnacle of Chinese art and culture, producing numerous talented thinkers, poets, and painters. Its capital, Bianjing (now Kaifeng city in Henan Province), was the largest and wealthiest city in the world at that time, with a population of over one million. The 528-centimeter-long painting captures the urban landscape and ways of life during the heyday of the Northern Song Dynasty in the 12th century. It has been passed on from generation to generation.

Along the River During the Qingming Festival centers around the Bian River, and features the countryside, the surroundings of a water and land transportation hub, and the market in the city center. Presented as a long scroll, the painting employs parallel projection, allowing for the depiction of over 500 people from all walks of life, including nobles, officials, servants, vendors, sedan bearers, laborers, storytellers, barbers, doctors, women, monks, children, beggars, and more. The painting's meticulous portrayal of daily life in the market, including animals, buildings, city walls, bridges, boats, vehicles, and sedan chairs, is unparalleled in its detail. The complexity is balanced with a concise and orderly composition, revealing

情趣。这在中国乃至世界绘画史上都是独一无二的。

《清明上河图》是一部北宋社会生活的百科全书，具有重要的历史文献价值和艺术价值。美国著名城市史学家刘易斯·芒福德因其景观生动多样化、人物属性各异而充满生机，将《清明上河图》作为未来城市理想的说明图。

a rich artistic charm that is unmatched in the history of Chinese and world painting.

Along the River During the Qingming Festival serves as a comprehensive encyclopedia of the social life of the Northern Song dynasty. It is of immense historical and artistic significance. Lewis Mumford, a renowned American historian who specialized in the study of cities, regarded the painting as an ideal model of the future city due to its vibrancy, variety, and focus on culture and people.

▲《清明上河图》(局部)
A part of the painting "Along the River during the Qingming Festival"

八大山人

朱耷（1626—1705），明末清初画家，号“八大山人”。他的绘画以大笔水墨写意而成，并善于泼墨，尤以花鸟画著称于世，在创作上取法自然、笔墨简练、形象夸张、独具新意。

八大山人画风、章法结构特立独行，在不完整中求完整，反映出一种孤傲落寞、愤世嫉俗的心境。例如，他画的鱼、鸭、鸟等，多以白眼向天，充满倔强之气，以此来表现自己遗世独立的操守。他笔墨不受空间表现规律制约，不去模仿其形，而是勾画意境，描绘心灵世界，并被后世尊为中国古典写意画的杰出大师，如清代的吴昌硕、近代的齐白石等著名画家，都深受其影响。

Bada Shanren

Zhu Da (1626-1705), also known as "Bada Shanren" (art or literary name), a painter who lived in the late Ming (1368-1644) and early Qing (1616-1911) dynasties. Being adept at using splash-ink techniques, Zhu Da created many freehand brush works, among which those with flowers or birds as themes are especially well-known. He owed his painting style to the spirit of nature, painting extravagant images with concise strokes, which are original and innovative.

Bada Shanren had a unique painting style and a special understanding of layouts and structure; he sought completeness from the incompleteness of what he painted, which reflected his aloof, proud and cynical mindset. For example, the fish, ducks and birds he painted are mostly rolling their eyes to the sky, posing obstinate gestures, which could mirror Bada Shanren's own solitude and moral integrity. His strokes were not restricted by any space rules in painting — instead of sketching the outer look of subjects, he highlighted the ideas and focused on expressing his inner world. Later generations consider Bada Shanren as a brilliant master of Chinese freehand brushwork. Wu Changshuo from the Qing Dynasty and Qi Baishi in contemporary times are among the famous painters who were deeply influenced by Bada Shanren.

剪纸艺术

剪纸是一种用剪刀或刻刀在纸上剪刻出各种造型、场景，以装点生活、表达特定寓意的民间艺术。

在纸张发明之前，人们往往在金银箔片上镂空雕刻各种图案花纹等，制成工艺品。西周时期，周成王将梧桐叶剪成玉圭的形状，这是中国古代有关剪纸艺术的最早文献记载。南北朝以后，剪纸艺术在民间逐渐盛行，出现了构图完整、手法多样的剪纸作品。宋代剪纸名目繁多，出现了贴于窗上的“窗花”和用于灯彩、茶盏的剪纸装饰。到了明清时期，剪纸艺术走向成熟，作为全民性艺术作品广泛用于家居装饰。近代以来至中华人民共和国成立后，剪纸创作内容更加丰富，各行各业生产生活和风俗民情等成为剪纸作品的常见题材。

Paper Cutting

Paper cutting is a folk art that involves using scissors or art knives to cut patterns and scenes in paper for decorative purposes or to convey specific meanings.

Before paper was invented, people used thin materials such as gold or silver foil to carve hollowed patterns to make art. The earliest written record of paper cutting in ancient China dates back to the Western Zhou Dynasty (1046-771 B.C.) when King Cheng of Zhou cut a parasol tree leaf into the shape of a jade gui (a ritual jade that symbolized statues). After the Northern and Southern dynasties (420-589), paper cutting gradually gained in popularity among the people, and various paper cutting works with complete compositions and utilizing different techniques came into existence. During the Song Dynasty (960-1279), different types of paper cuts were created, including those used to adorn windows, lanterns, and tea cups. The art of paper cutting reached its peak in the Ming (1368-1644) and Qing (1616-1911) dynasties. Paper cuts were used to decorate almost anything, especially for interior decor. In modern times, especially since the founding of the People's Republic of China, the contents of paper cutting have been enriched, incorporating the everyday life and work of all walks of life and folk customs as common themes.

剪纸艺术善于把多种物体形象组合在一起，代表不同寓意，表达美好愿望。比如，仙鹤、松树象征长寿；娃娃、葫芦、莲花等图案象征多子多福。春节时，当年生肖的剪纸窗花就十分常见。随着时代发展，民间出现了用套色点染等方法制作的彩色剪纸，强化了剪纸作品的表现力。剪纸艺术还形成了不同的流派与风格，如中国北方派作品豪放粗犷，南方派风格婉约细腻。

在中国历史上，剪纸艺术自诞生以来从未中断，它交融于各族人民的社会生活，是各种民俗活动的重要组成部分，也是民间手工艺术的重要形态。2009年，“中国剪纸”列入联合国教科文组织人类非物质文化遗产代表作名录。

The art of paper cutting is known for its ability to combine images of various objects to represent different meanings and express good wishes. For example, cranes and pine trees are symbols of longevity, while patterns of babies, gourds (which sound similar to the Chinese characters fu and lu, meaning "happiness" and "good fortune"), and lotus flowers symbolize blessings and fertility. During the Spring Festival, it is common to use paper cuts of the Chinese zodiac animal of that year to decorate windows. Gradually, colored paper-cutting made with shading and dyeing methods has emerged, making the art of paper cutting more expressive. The art has developed different schools and styles. The northern school is bold and unconstrained, while the southern school is graceful and elegant.

The art of paper cutting has continued to evolve. It has been integrated into the social life of all ethnic groups, becoming an integral part of various folk activities. It is also an important folk handicraft. In 2009, Chinese paper-cutting was added to the Representative List of the Intangible Cultural Heritage of Humanity by UNESCO.

唐卡

唐卡是藏文音译，是一种用刺绣或绘制等手法在布、绢、纸上创作的彩色卷轴画，是中国藏族文化中一种独具特色的艺术形式，具有鲜明的民族特色和浓郁的宗教色彩。

唐卡尺寸大小不一，构图严谨、均衡，色彩明亮、饱满，绘制程序严苛、复杂。唐卡绘制颜料传统上全部采用金、珍珠、玛瑙、松石、孔雀石等珍贵的矿物宝石和植物颜料，这些天然原料保证了唐卡色泽鲜艳，璀璨夺目，经久不变色。

唐卡的题材内容以佛教为主，涉及历史、政治、经济、文化、民俗、建筑、医学、天文、历法等领域，具有宗教性、艺术性、知识性等，堪称“藏文化的大百科全书”。

Tangka

"Tangka" is a term that has been transliterated from Tibetan. It refers to a colorful scroll painting created using embroidery or painting techniques on cloth, silk, or paper. This unique art form is deeply rooted in China's Tibetan culture, and it is characterized by distinct ethnic features and strong religious hues.

Tangkas vary in size. They feature meticulous and harmonious compositions, as well as vibrant and saturated colors. The painting process is highly demanding and intricate. The pigments used in tangkas are traditionally sourced from precious minerals and gems such as gold, pearls, turquoise, and malachite, as well as plants. This creates a breathtaking, vivid, and long-lasting color palette that can endure for centuries.

Thangkas are primarily focused on themes related to Buddhism. They cover a wide range of subjects, including history, politics, economy, culture, folklore, architecture, medicine, astronomy and the calendar. Tangkas possess qualities such as religious, artistic, and educational significance, and are often referred to as the "Encyclopedia of Tibetan culture."

五音十二律

五音十二律是中国传统乐律学名词，是中国古代的定音方法。五音，即宫、商、角、徵、羽，是中国古代音乐的基本音阶。“五音”最早出自春秋时期的典籍，如《左传》《周礼》《管子》之中。中国古人把“五音”同“五行”相对应（见图表），形成了独特的音乐理论体系。

五音	宫	商	角	徵	羽
五行	土	金	木	火	水
唱名	do	re	mi	sol	la

中国古人提出了“十二律”的定音方法，即用三分损益法将一个八度分为十二个不完全相同的半音的一种律制。1584年，朱载堉利用新的数学方法，用特大算盘进行开方计算，研究出十二平均律的关键数据——$\sqrt[12]{2}$，并以此为据，设计并制造出两种定音乐器。朱载堉发现的“十二平均律”在世界律学史上属首创，解决了音乐领域的千古学术难题。

Five tones and 12 pitches

The five tones and 12 pitches are terms in traditional Chinese music, which refer to the ancient Chinese method of tuning. The five tones – gong, shang, jue, zhi and yu – form the basic scales of ancient Chinese music. The term "five tones" first appeared in ancient Chinese literature during the Spring and Autumn period (770-476 B.C.), in works such as *Zuo Zhuan* (*Commentary on the Spring and Autumn Annals*), *Rites of Zhou*, and *Guanzi*. The ancient Chinese connected the five tones of Chinese scales with the five elements, or wuxing (as shown in the chart), resulting in a unique system of music theory.

five tones	gong	shang	jue	zhi	yu
five elements	earth	metal	wood	fire	Water
solfege names	do	re	mi	sol	La

The ancient Chinese proposed the 12 pitches tonal system, which used the "Method of dividing into three parts and taking away one part" to divide an octave into 12 different semitone pitches. In 1584, Zhu Zaiyu used a new mathematical method to calculate square roots using an extra-large abacus to derive a critical ratio equal to the 12th root of 2, which was instrumental in the development of the "12-tone equal temperament." Based on these findings, he designed and developed two types of tuning instruments. Zhu's ingenious method of arithmetic calculation of equal temperament was the first in the history of world temperament, which solved a long-standing problem in the field of music.

编钟

中国是世界上最早制造和使用乐钟的国家。编钟作为中国古代大型打击乐器，最早出现于商朝，盛于春秋战国直至秦汉，集中体现了中国传统礼乐文化。每逢征战、宴享、朝聘、祭祀，都要演奏编钟。

编钟用青铜铸成，钟身有精美图案，大小不同的铜钟按照音调高低依序排列，悬挂在一个巨大的钟架上，用丁字形的木锤和长形的棒分别敲打铜钟，能发出不同的乐音。编钟一般与编磬（一种石头磨制而成的乐器）配合使用，多运用于庄严肃穆的庙堂宫廷雅乐场合。西周时期，编钟多由大小3枚铜钟组合起来。春秋战国时期，编钟数目逐渐增至9枚或13枚一组。编钟的发声原理是钟体小则音调高、音量小，钟体大则音调低、音量大，因而其铸造尺寸和形状一定程度上决定了编钟的发音。

Bianzhong

China was the first country to create and utilize musical chimes, with the *bianzhong*, or chime bells, being a notable example of these instruments. The *bianzhong* is a large ancient percussion instrument that originated during the Shang Dynasty (1600-1046 B.C.) and flourished in the Spring and Autumn period (770-476 B.C.) and the Warring States period (475-221 B.C.) as well as Qin (221-206 B.C.) and Han (206 B.C. - A.D. 220) dynasties, representing China's traditional ceremonial music culture. The *bianzhong* were played during occasions such as military expeditions, festivals, court audiences for nobility, and sacrificial ceremonies.

Crafted from bronze, the *bianzhong* features exquisite patterns on the body of the bells. Bronze bells of various sizes are arranged in order of pitch on a large bell frame and are struck by musicians using T-shaped wooden mallets and rods to create different pitches. The *bianzhong* is typically accompanied by the *bianqing*, a percussion instrument made of polished stone. They are primarily played during solemn ritual ceremonies at imperial altars. During the Western Zhou Dynasty (1046-771 B.C.), the *bianzhong* were commonly arranged in sets of three, and later in the Spring and Autumn period and the Warring States period, they were increasingly grouped in sets of nine or 13. The smaller bells produce high-pitched tones and softer sounds, while larger bells produce deeper and louder notes. The size and shape of the bells determine the specific sounds they produce.

战国时代曾侯乙墓（约前433）出土的编钟最引人注目，它由65个钟组成，总音域横跨五个八度，中心音域十二个半音齐全。与现代钢琴相比，它仅在最低、最高音处各少一个八度，几乎能够演奏现代所有乐曲。曾侯乙编钟上三千多字的铭文是世界文明史上最早的有声音乐理论文献，以声音和文字互相印证的方式，保存了2400年前的音乐记忆，代表了中国先秦礼乐文明与青铜器铸造技术的最高成就。

编钟作为一种古老的打击乐器，展现了中国古代音乐文化的先进水平，其在音质、音准、音色方面不逊于当代民族打击乐器和西洋打击乐器。1957年，由河南信阳出土的最早的青铜编钟演奏的《东方红》乐曲，随着中国第一颗人造卫星发射升空，在浩瀚宇宙中发出了穿越时空的中国声音。

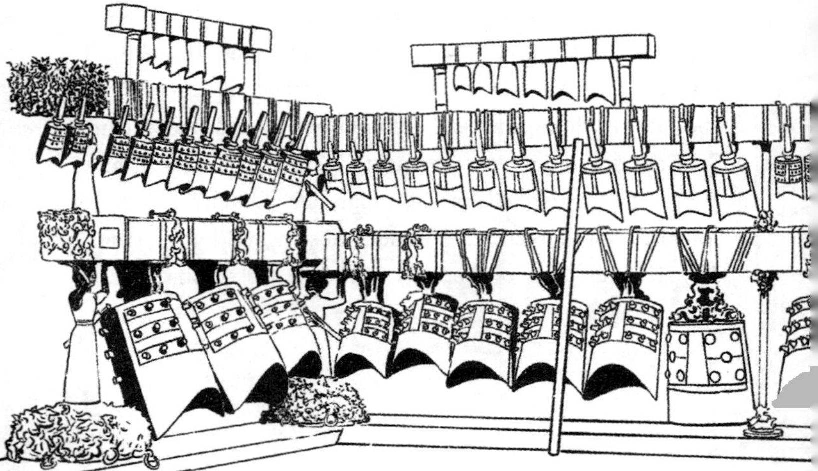

One of the most remarkable *bianzhong* was unearthed from the tomb of Marquis Yi of Zeng (c. 433 B.C.) in the Warring States period. It consists of 65 bells and has a tonal range of five octaves. In the middle area of the tonal range, it can play all twelve half tones. Compared to a modern piano, it only lacks one octave at the lowest and highest ends and can play almost all modern music. The 3,000+ characters inscribed on the *bianzhong* bells of the Marquis Yi of Zeng constitute the earliest known text on music theory in the world history. It preserves musical lore from 2,400 years ago through sound and text, representing the highest achievements in the pre-Qin period of ancient China in ritual music and bronze casting technology.

The *bianzhong* demonstrates the advanced level of ancient Chinese music culture. Its sound quality, pitch accuracy, and timbre match those of contemporary ethnic percussion instruments and Western percussion instruments. In 1957, as China's first man-made satellite was launched into space, the song "The East is Red" was broadcast, played by the first bronze *bianzhong* unearthed in Xinyang of Henan Province. The music transcended time and space, echoing throughout the vast universe, and bringing the sound of China to the world.

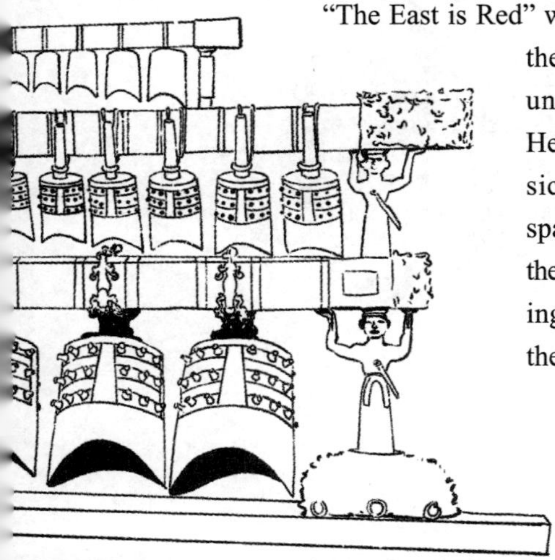

古琴

古琴是中国最古老的一种弹拨乐器，一般由梧桐木做箱体，用蚕丝做弦，造型优美，音域宽广，音色深沉，余音悠远，代表高雅之趣。20世纪初，为了与西方传入的钢琴相区别，才被称作“古琴”。

中国古琴文化源远流长，距今有3000多年历史。古籍记载琴的创制与上古时期部落联盟首领有关，有伏羲作琴、黄帝造琴等传说。西周时期的钟仪是现存记载中最早的专业琴人。战国时期音乐家俞伯牙和钟子期“《高山》《流水》觅知音”的故事，成为广为流传的佳话美谈，琴台也被视为友谊的象征。

Guqin

The *guqin* is the oldest plucked string instrument in China. Crafted with a soundboard usually made of the Chinese parasol tree (firmiana simplex) wood and strings made of silk, the instrument has an elegant appearance and produces a distinctive sound that is deep, lingering, ethereal, and calming. It has long been considered an instrument of great subtlety and refinement. In the early 20th century, it was named as such to differentiate it from the piano, which arrived from the West.

The culture of the *guqin* in China has a history that spans over 3,000 years. According to ancient books, the invention of the *guqin* was associated with tribal leaders in ancient China. Legend has it that Fuxi and Huangdi (Yellow Emperor) were involved in its creation, while Zhong Yi, a musician of the Western Zhou period (1046-771 B.C.), is the earliest recorded professional player. The story of musicians Yu Boya and Zhong Ziqi in the Warring States period is a popular legend about music and friendship. The two musicians made their acquaintance and developed their friendship through the *guqin* pieces *Lofty Mountains* and *Flowing Rivers*. The *guqin* table, as a result, has been regarded as a symbol of friendship.

琴是中国古代文化地位最崇高的乐器，位列“琴、棋、书、画”四艺之首，自古以来一直是许多文人必修的知识技能。古琴因其清、和、淡、雅的音乐品格寄寓了文人超凡脱俗的处世心态。隋唐时期，古琴传入东亚诸国；近代又伴随着华人的足迹走向世界各地。古琴音乐作为中国古典音乐的精髓和人类代表性艺术成果，曾铸刻在1977年美国“旅行者”号行星探测器的镀金唱片里，在茫茫宇宙中传播中国古典音乐的高雅之声。2003年，“古琴艺术”列入联合国教科文组织人类非物质文化遗产代表作名录。

The *guqin* has long been regarded as the crown of all musical instruments in traditional Chinese culture, topping the list of the four essential arts that Chinese scholars were expected to master, the other three being chess, calligraphy, and painting. The pure, serene, elegant and refined character of *guqin* music reflects the literati's extraordinary and unique approach to life. It spread to other East Asian countries during the Sui (581-618) and Tang (618-907) dynasties and has since further spread throughout the world with the more recent migrations of the Chinese. In 1977, as a quintessential art form in traditional Chinese music, a piece of *guqin* music was taken aboard the Voyager 2 spacecraft sent by the United States into space, spreading the elegant sound of Chinese classical music throughout the vast universe. In 2003, the *guqin* and its music were inscribed on the Representative List of the Intangible Cultural Heritage of Humanity by UNESCO.

昆曲

昆曲是中国古老的戏曲声腔、剧种，起源于14世纪元末明初的江苏昆山地区，后经顾坚（约1368）等人整理加工，明嘉靖年间又经魏良辅（1489—1566）改良后走向全国，成为中国传统戏剧艺术中最重要的一种戏剧形式。

昆曲表演注重身段动作的优美与音乐的和谐，伴奏乐器以曲笛为主，辅以笙、箫等，角色分工细致。其剧目丰富多彩，以传奇为主，唱词华丽典雅，曲调清柔婉转，舞姿细腻优美，武功技术卓绝，表演情真意切，具有诗的意境、画的风采，融诗、乐、歌、舞、戏于一体的艺术表现形式，堪称戏曲表演的最高境界，对中国近代戏剧发展产生巨大影响。流传至今的昆曲代表性剧目有《牡丹亭》《玉簪记》《长生殿》等。

昆曲表演艺术是中国戏曲艺术的精华，在中国戏曲史、

Kunqu

Kunqu, an ancient form of Chinese opera dating back to the 14th century during the late Yuan (1206-1368) and early Ming (1368-1644) dynasties, originated in the Kunshan region of Jiangsu province. It was refined and developed by Gu Jian and others (c. 1368). During the Jiajing reign of the Ming Dynasty, Wei Liangfu (1489-1566) further refined *Kunqu*, enabling it to achieve national recognition as the most esteemed form of Chinese drama.

Kunqu's exquisite performances emphasize graceful movements and harmonious music. The primary instrument in the *Kunqu* orchestra is the *qudi*, a bamboo flute with bone end-caps. The orchestra also employs other instruments, such as the *sheng*, a mouth-blown polyphonic free reed instrument, and the *xiao*, a vertical end-blown flute. Roles in *Kunqu* plays are thoughtfully designed for each performer, and the repertoire covers a broad range of genres, with legends being the most popular. The performances involve elegant lyrics, melodious music, delicate dances, and impressive martial arts skills. *Kunqu's* artistry involves poetry, music, singing, dance, and theater, and is regarded as the highest form of traditional Chinese drama. *Kunqu* has greatly influenced the development of modern Chinese drama, and several notable plays, such as *The Peony Pavilion*, *The Jade Hairpin*, and *The Palace of Eternal Life*, have been passed down to the present day.

As the quintessential form of Chinese opera, *Kunqu* holds a significant place in the history of Chinese theatre, literature,

文学史、音乐史上都占有重要的地位，享有“百戏之祖”的美誉。2008年，“昆曲”列入联合国教科文组织人类非物质文化遗产代表作名录。

and music. It is revered as the "mother of Chinese operas." In 2008, *Kunqu* was included in the Representative List of the Intangible Cultural Heritage of Humanity by UNESCO.

京剧

中国国粹京剧是一种融合唱、念、做、打的表演艺术，融汇徽剧、汉调、昆曲、秦腔及其他地方民间曲调，并结合北京的语言特点而形成。京剧自1840年至1860年之间形成并流传至今，是中国影响最大的戏曲剧种，也是中华民族传统文化的重要表现形式，享有中国“国剧”的美誉。

京剧以历史故事为主要演出内容，在剧本、表演、音乐、舞台美术等各个方面都有一套规范化的艺术表现形式，著名剧目有《霸王别姬》《空城计》《智取威虎山》等。京剧的主要声腔为二黄、西皮，伴奏分胡琴、长笛主奏的文场和班鼓、大锣主奏的武场两大类。现今流行的京剧角色主要分为生、旦、净、丑四种，其中，“生”是除了花脸和丑角以外的男性正面角色的统称，分老生、武生、小生；“旦”是

Peking Opera

Peking Opera is a performance art that integrates singing, recital, acting, and martial arts, with the first two being song forms and the last two being dance forms. The dramatic artistic effects are achieved through routines of hand, eye, body, and foot movements.

With roots dating back to 1840-1860, Peking Opera assimilated various local folk music styles such as Hui, Han, Kunqu, and Shaanxi operas. The performers primarily sing and recite in the Beijing dialect. Today, Peking Opera is the most popular and influential form of stage performance in China and an important representation of traditional Chinese culture. It is widely regarded as the national opera of China.

Peking Opera's repertoire primarily draws from Chinese history. It has standardized artistic expressions in text, performance, music, and set designs. Famous plays include *Farewell My Concubine*, *The Ruse of the Empty City*, and *Taking Tiger Mountain by Strategy*. The vocal music mainly consists of *erhuang* (adapted from folk tunes of Anhui and Hubei) and *xipi* (from Shaanxi tunes). Accompanying these are two types of instruments: *wenchang* (civilian plays) with *huqin* (a two-stringed fiddle) and flute, and *wuchang* (martial plays) with *bangu* (a Chinese frame drum) and big gong. The characters in Peking Opera are generally divided into four types of roles: the *sheng* (male roles), *dan* (female roles), *jing* (male roles with painted face), and *chou* (clown or a negative character). The *sheng* includes positive male roles excluding the *hualian* (the

女性正面角色的统称，分青衣（正旦）、花旦、闺门旦、刀马旦、武旦、彩旦、老旦；“净”大多是性格、品质或相貌上有些特异的男性人物，化妆用脸谱，音色洪亮，风格粗犷；“丑”扮演喜剧角色，故在鼻梁上抹一小块白粉。脸谱是京剧的鲜明特色，红脸代表忠勇，黑脸代表智猛，蓝脸和绿脸代表草莽英雄，黄脸和白脸代表狡诈凶恶，金脸和银脸代表神妖。京剧表演的艺术手法中，唱和念属于“歌”，做和打属于“舞”，它们通过既定的手、眼、身、脚动作编排实现戏剧艺术效果。

中华人民共和国成立后，京剧作为国家文化使者在海外广泛传播并深受赞誉，以京剧艺术大师梅兰芳为代表的京剧海外演出改变了当时西方民众对中国文化的偏见，增进了中西方文化交流，对东亚、欧美的戏剧和电影艺术发展产生深

mighty character with heavily painted face) and *chou* and is further divided into *laosheng* (a dignified older role), *wusheng* (a martial character for roles involving combat), and *xiaosheng* (young male character). The *dan* refers to any positive female role and includes *qingyi/zhengdan* (virtuous and elite women), *huadan* (vivacious and unmarried women), *guimendan* (young, good-looking woman from a wealthy family), *daomadan/wudan* (young female warriors), *caidan* (clownish and cunning females), and *laodan* (old women). The *jing* mainly refers to male characters with unique personalities or appearances. This category features colorful make-up and low, powerful voices, full of primal energy. A *chou*, depicted by a patch of white on the face, is a humorous character. Facial makeup is a distinctive feature of Peking opera, with red representing loyalty and bravery, black representing wisdom and fierceness, blue and green representing grass-roots heroes, yellow and white representing cunning and wickedness, and gold and silver representing gods and spirits.

Since the founding of the People's Republic of China, Peking Opera has been widely promoted overseas and is highly regarded as a cultural envoy. Peking Opera performances by master artists like Mei Lanfang have helped remedy Western biases against Chinese culture, promoted cultural exchanges between China and the West, and had a profound impact on the development of theater and film arts in East Asia, Europe and the United States. The Peking Opera performance system

远影响。梅兰芳京剧表演体系被视为东方戏剧表演体系的代表。2010年，“京剧”列入联合国教科文组织人类非物质文化遗产代表作名录。

named after Mei Lanfang is recognized as a representative of the oriental drama performing systems. In 2010, Peking Opera was inscribed on the Representative List of the Intangible Cultural Heritage of Humanity by UNESCO.

变脸

变脸是中国传统戏剧中塑造人物的一种特技，通过瞬间改变脸谱，表现人物内心的情感变化，令人拍案叫绝。

变脸表演要求动作敏捷、不露痕迹，对演员技巧要求较高。变脸可以给观众一种不同于其他戏曲表演的体验和感受，具有极强的感染力。中国不少剧种中都有变脸特技，其中以川剧中的变脸最为著名。川剧变脸主要有抹暴眼、吹粉、扯脸等手法。抹暴眼是演员手指抹上预存于眉头或鬓的墨青，一抹即变；吹粉是演员吹起色粉，事先在需要变化的地方涂油，以改变脸色，抹暴眼和吹粉都属于涂面化妆。扯脸则需要将脸谱面具一层层地贴套在脸上，且松紧有度，在剧情需要时一个个拉下来达到变脸效果。

变脸作为中华传统文化的一张名片，多次在国际舞台上展示中国传统戏剧的技艺绝活和独特风采，获得各国人民的广泛赞誉。

Face-changing

Face-changing is a special technique for building characters in traditional Chinese opera. By changing faces in the blink of an eye, performers could express the emotional changes of their characters.

Face-changing requires dexterity and smooth and subtle movements. It achieves intended effects to appeal to the audience in a way different from other performing skills in traditional Chinese opera. The use of this technique, though widespread in many opera genres, is most prominent in Sichuan Opera, in which face-changing takes place through plastering, powder-blowing, or facemask-switching. Plastering refers to the move by which performers smear part of their faces using cosmetic paint previously hidden in eyebrows or hair. Powder-blowing is applied to change the colors of performers' faces. This requires performers to oil their faces in the area that needs color-change in advance, so that colored powder will stick after being blown to their faces. Aside from face coloring, mask switching allows performers to change faces instantly. They attach make-up masks to their faces in layers, neither too tight nor too loose, and when the cue comes, they pull the masks off one by one.

Face-changing is a technique unique to traditional Chinese culture and has won plaudits in countries around the world where traditional Chinese operas are performed.

皮影戏

皮影戏，就是以皮制或纸制的彩色影偶形象，伴随音乐和演唱进行表演的一种戏剧形式，是中国民间传统艺术。皮影戏艺人在幕后用木杆操控影偶，通过光线照射在半透明的幕布上创造出动态的形象，具有独特的艺术效果。

皮影戏始于西汉时期，兴于唐代，在宋代成熟和盛行，元代传至西亚和欧洲，到清代呈现全国流行的繁荣局面。在电影电视没有普及的时代，皮影戏深受中国各地民众欢迎，在长期演化过程中形成了不同的艺术流派。

皮影的艺术创意汲取了中国汉代帛画、画像石、画像砖和唐、宋寺院壁画的手法与风格。表演时，艺人一边紧贴幕

Shadow Puppetry

Shadow Puppetry is a form of traditional Chinese folk art that uses colored leather or paper silhouette figures that perform to music and song. During the performance, puppeteers manipulate the figures using wooden rods to create an effect of moving images on a translucent cloth screen that is illuminated from behind, creating a unique artistic effect.

Shadow Puppetry dates back to the Western Han Dynasty (206 B.C. - A.D. 25). It flourished during the Tang Dynasty (618-907), matured and gained popularity during the Song Dynasty (960-1279), and spread to Western Asia and Europe during the Yuan Dynasty (1206-1368). By the Qing Dynasty (1616-1911) it had become a popular art form throughout the country. Over time, it evolved into different artistic schools. Shadow Puppetry retained its popularity before the advent of film and television.

Shadow Puppetry draws on the techniques and styles of silk paintings, portrait stones, and portrait bricks of the Han Dynasty (206 B.C.- A.D. 220), as well as temple murals from the Tang and Song dynasties. During the performance, the pup-

布操控影偶肢体活动，真切地表现各种复杂的场景，一边用当地流行的曲调唱出故事内容，同时配以打击乐和弦乐，声情并茂、动人心弦。皮影戏常见剧目有《白蛇传》《杨家将》《西游记》等。

皮影戏传递文化历史、社会信仰、口头传统和当地风俗等信息，在知识传播和文化交流中发挥积极作用，入选人类非物质文化遗产代表作名录。这种源于中国的民间艺术形式，吸引了许多国外戏迷，被称为神奇的“中国影子”“东方魔术般的艺术”“电影的鼻祖”。

peteer manipulates the puppet's movements against the screen, bringing to life various complex scenes on the screen with remarkable vividness. At the same time, the puppeteer sings the story using popular local melodies, accompanied by percussion and stringed instruments, resulting in an interesting and entertaining performance. Some of the most popular Shadow puppetry plays include *The Legend of the White Snake*, *Female Generals of the Yang Family*, and *Journey to the West*.

Shadow Puppetry passes on culture, folk beliefs, oral traditions and local customs. It spreads knowledge and promotes cultural exchange. Chinese Shadow Puppetry has been included in the Representative List of the Intangible Cultural Heritage of Humanity. This form of folk art has a global following, with foreign admirers referring to it as "Chinese shadow", "Eastern magical art", and "Ancestor of cinema".

围棋

围棋是中国传统棋种，古称“弈”，相传为上古时期部落首领尧所发明，是世界上最古老的棋类游戏。中国围棋历史已有4000年以上。

围棋是两人对局，有棋盘和棋子。棋盘上有横竖各19条平行线，构成361个交叉点。棋子为扁圆形，分黑白两种，黑子为181枚，白子为180枚。古时，围棋作为一项重要的文化娱乐活动，在文人和士大夫中较为流行。他们将“琴、棋、书、画”四者相提并论，认为围棋是一个反映智慧、体现志趣的高雅艺术。

围棋是中国历史上对外文化交流的重要内容。隋唐以后，围棋先后传入朝鲜、日本等国，并逐渐传播到世界各地。如今，围棋已成为国际体育领域智力竞技的重要项目。

Go

Go is a traditional Chinese board game. It was referred to as "yi" in ancient times. Legends trace the game's origin back more than 4,000 years to the mythical Chinese emperor Yao, making it the oldest board game in the world.

Go is a two-player game played with a board and pieces. The board is marked with 19 parallel vertical lines and 19 parallel horizontal lines, forming 361 points. The pieces used in the game are flat underneath and convex on top, and they come in two colors, black and white. The players have at their disposal 181 black pieces and 180 white pieces. There are various formats, including occupying territory and drawing unbroken lines. In ancient times Go held significant cultural and recreational value, and was popular among literati and scholars. They regarded music, chess, calligraphy, and painting as the four essential arts, and considered Go to be an elegant activity that reflects intelligence and personality.

Go holds a crucial place in the history of China's cultural exchanges with foreign countries. From the Sui (581-618) and Tang (618-907) dynasties, the game was introduced to Korea, Japan, and other countries and gradually spread to various parts of the world. Today, Go has become an important intellectual sport in the international sports arena.

中国象棋

中国象棋是中国传统棋种，为区别于国际象棋，故称中国象棋。其起源被认为与军事有着密切关系，是模仿两军对垒的一种谋略游戏。

中国象棋是两人对局，有棋盘、棋子。棋盘由9道直线和10道横线交叉组成，共有90个交叉点。棋盘中间没有画线的地方是双方的分界线，名为“楚河汉界”，画有米字斜交叉线的方形区域是安放将帅的“九宫”。棋子分红、黑两组，各16子。古人认为，中国象棋不仅具有娱乐作用，而且可以启迪智慧，培养战略思维，锻炼指挥能力。

中国象棋是中国最普及、最受欢迎的棋类游戏之一。自唐朝起，中国象棋开始向日本、朝鲜、越南等地广泛传播，清朝后期传播到欧美，逐渐走向世界。

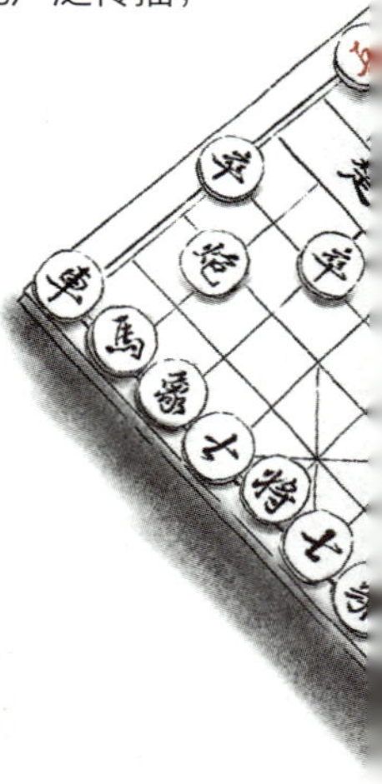

Chinese Chess

Chinese Chess is a traditional board game. It is so named in order to be distinguished from international chess. Like international chess, it is a strategy game that simulates the confrontation between two armies and is believed to have roots in military strategy.

Chinese Chess is a two-player game played with a board and pieces. The board has 90 intersections formed by nine vertical lines and 10 horizontal lines. The thick horizontal line in the middle of the board which separates the two sides is called the "River of the Chu and Border of the Han". The square zones containing diagonal lines are the palaces where the generals are placed. The pieces are divided into two groups, red and black, with 16 pieces for each player. The ancient Chinese saw Chinese Chess as a means to inspire wisdom, cultivate strategic thinking, and demonstrate leadership ability in addition to a form of entertainment.

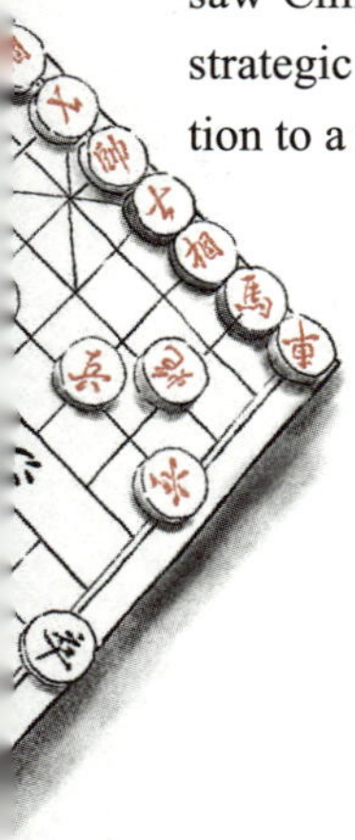

Chinese Chess is one of the most popular board games in China. Following the Tang Dynasty (618-907), the game was introduced to other Asian countries such as Japan, Korea, and Vietnam. In the late Qing Dynasty (1616-1911) it spread to Europe and America, gradually becoming a worldwide game.

太极拳

太极拳是一种强调内外兼修的中国传统武术拳法，既可养气强身、用于技击，又有保健医疗的作用。太极拳创始于明末清初，山西武术家王宗岳（1736—1795）用太极阴阳的哲理来解释拳理，写成《太极拳论》，“太极拳”由此定名。在长期发展中，太极拳形成了陈式、杨式、吴式等多种流派，是中国传统武术的集大成者。

太极拳将传统阴阳学说、太极理论融入到拳法中，讲究意、气、形、神的统一。太极拳认为，人的身心是一体的，人只有静下心来，身体才会真正放松，从而获得健康和愉悦。太极拳要求注意力集中和身心宁静，强调动作连贯圆活、刚柔并济，讲究以静制动、以柔克刚、避实就虚、借力发力，展现伸展与协调、稳健和均匀的特点。

太极拳不仅在中华大地久盛不衰，在世界范围内也得

Taijiquan (Tai Chi Boxing)

Taijiquan (Tai Chi Boxing) is a traditional Chinese martial art that emphasizes the cultivation of both internal and external strength. It can be used for health benefits, self-defense, and therapeutic purposes. Taijiquan was created during the late Ming (1368-1644) and early Qing (1616-1911) dynasties by Wang Zongyue (1736-1795), a martial artist from Shanxi province. Wang expounded upon the principles of the art using the traditional Chinese philosophy of Yin and Yang and wrote a book titled *On Taijiquan*, thus giving the art its name. Over time, Taijiquan has evolved into various styles that are named after either a clan or a master, such as the Chen Style, Yang Style, and Wu Style. It is a leading form of traditional Chinese martial arts.

Taijiquan incorporates traditional Yin-Yang theory and Taiji (Tai Chi) principles into martial arts, emphasizing the unity of intention, energy, body, and mind. It teaches that the mind and body are interconnected, and health and happiness can be achieved by calming the mind through relaxing the body. Taijiquan requires the practitioner to maintain focused attention and a state of mental tranquility. It places great emphasis on smooth and fluid movements that balance hardness with softness. Taijiquan also emphasizes utilizing softness to conquer hardness and stillness to defeat motion. It advocates strategies such as avoiding brute force and instead diverting the opponent's attacks to turn their own force against them. Practicing Taijiquan can help with stretching, coordination, stability, and balance.

Taijiquan has long been popular in China and has now

到了广泛传播，成为促进中外文化交流的重要纽带。2020年，“太极拳”列入联合国教科文组织人类非物质文化遗产代表作名录。

widely spread around the world. It serves as a significant cultural bridge, promoting exchanges between China and other nations. In 2020, Taijiquan was added to the Representative List of the Intangible Cultural Heritage of Humanity the UNESCO.

少林功夫

少林功夫，亦即少林拳，是中国武术界各大流派中历史最悠久、种类最繁多、体系最庞大、最具文化内涵的门派。少林功夫发源于河南嵩山的少林寺。相传南北朝时期，印度高僧达摩（？—536）曾来此传授禅宗、静坐修心。达摩等人仿效中国古代劳动人民锻炼身体的各种动作，编成健身活动的“活身法”以及动静结合的“十八罗汉手”以传授僧人，形成“少林拳”的雏形。1500多年来，少林功夫有序传承、从未间断，由最初保护寺院、强身健体的手段，逐渐发展成为技术完备、内涵丰富的文化表现形式。历代传习的少林功夫套路有数百种，其中较为流传的有拳术、棍术、刀术、剑术、器械和对练等。随着社会发展，少林功夫已经演变为一种具有独特功能的体育运动项目。

Shaolin Kung Fu

Shaolin Kung Fu, also known as Shaolin Boxing, is the oldest martial art among all the major schools in China. It boasts the most diverse and comprehensive range of styles and the most profound cultural significance within the Chinese martial arts community. Its origins can be traced back to the Shaolin Temple in Songshan, Henan Province. According to legend, during the Southern and Northern dynasties (420-589) period, an Indian Buddhist monk named Bodhidharma (?-536) came to the Temple to teach Zen Buddhism and practice meditation. Bodhidharma, along with others, observed various movements performed by ancient Chinese individuals during physical exercise and adapted these movements to create a fitness routine called "body-relaxing techniques" and Luohan's 18 hands, with the latter combining dynamic and static elements. These forms of physical exercise were used to train monks and are considered the embryonic form of Shaolin Boxing. For over 1,500 years, Shaolin Kung Fu has been passed down consistently without interruption. From its origins as a means of protecting the temple and strengthening the body, it has gradually developed into a manifestation of culture with rich connotations and a complete set of wellness techniques. Throughout the ages, hundreds of Shaolin Kung Fu forms have been passed down, including popular training routines such as fighting or sparring with fists, with a stick, with a sword, or with other similar weapons. It has evolved into a unique sports activity with distinct features.

少林功夫具有完整的技术和理论体系，它以武术技艺和套路为表现形式，以佛教信仰和禅宗智慧为文化内涵，讲求“禅武合一”的精神境界，反映了“天人合一”的文化理念。对于智慧与力量的渴望，将禅修融入练武的过程，一直是少林功夫习练者的追求目标。这是少林功夫的特色所在，也是少林功夫与其他武术的主要区别。2006年，少林功夫入选中国国家级非物质文化遗产保护名录。

少林功夫有着增进和谐、健康向上的内容，其蕴含的慈悲、平等、圆融、和合理念，受到世界各国民众的关注与喜爱，吸引全球6000余万人习练功夫，从中获得身心裨益。少林寺在全球各地建立了200多个海外少林文化中心，以中华传统武术文化为媒介，促进中外文明交流互鉴。

The practice of Shaolin Kung Fu is based on a complete set of theories which infuse Buddhist beliefs, particularly Zen Buddhism, into martial arts techniques. The cultural concept of the "unity of heaven and man" is reflected in the emphasis on the "unity of Zen and martial arts". For Shaolin Kung Fu practitioners, the pursuit of wisdom and strength is inseparable from the integration of Zen meditation into the process of martial arts training. This is where Shaolin Kung Fu stands out from other martial arts. Shaolin Kung Fu was included on China's national intangible cultural heritage list in 2006.

Shaolin Kung Fu focuses on promoting harmony, health, compassion, equality, unity, and a positive lifestyle. These ideas have been embraced by people all over the world. More than 60 million people worldwide have benefited from practicing Shaolin Kung Fu. The Shaolin Temple has established more than 200 overseas cultural centers around the world, using traditional Chinese martial arts as a means to promote cross-cultural exchanges and mutual learning.

日常生活

Everyday life

热气腾腾的日常生活，永远是文学艺术、思想文化的不竭源泉。“舌尖上的中国”让人怦然心动，其背后是博大精深的中华饮食文化；此外还有服饰文化、建筑文化、民俗文化等，共同构成中华传统文化的器物层面。而春节、清明、中秋等中国传统节日，为中国人的日常生活带来稳定的节奏感，也造就了诸多特色鲜明的文化符号。“人间烟火气，最抚凡人心”。对于世俗生活的珍惜与重视，恰是中华文化的一大特色。

The hustle and bustle of everyday life provides an inexhaustible source of inspiration for literature, art, and cultural ideas. The success of the food and culture documentary "A Bite of China" can be attributed in part to people's love of China's rich culinary culture. While culinary culture, along with other cultural forms such as clothing, architecture, and folk traditions, represents the tangible aspect of traditional Chinese culture, traditional festivals, including the Spring Festival, Qingming Festival, and Mid-Autumn Festival, are intangible heritage with distinctive cultural symbols, which embed rhythm in people's lives. Celebrating daily commonplaces touches the heart the most. In Chinese culture, there is a deep appreciation for the simplest aspects of life.

筷子

筷子是中国饮食文化的标志之一，也是世界上常用餐具之一。中国人使用筷子至少有3000年历史。对中国人来说，筷子不只是常用的餐具，还承载着丰富的传统文化内涵：筷子两根为一双，中国人在使用筷子夹菜时，是一根主动，主动的为阳，一根从动，从动的为阴，这体现了阴阳学说；筷子的标准长度是七寸六分，代表人有七情六欲；筷子一头方一头圆，体现了“天圆地方”的传统观念。

自古代起，筷子逐渐流传到周边国家，成为东亚、东南亚地区许多国家的进餐工具。最早把筷子介绍到欧洲的是意大利人利玛窦（1552—1610），现在西方很多家庭都备有筷子，在德国还有一所“筷子博物馆”，里面收藏有上千种不同历史时期的筷子。今天，使用筷子不再是中国人的专利，筷子已经成为传递东方饮食文化的独特载体。

Chopsticks

Chopsticks are a symbol of Chinese culinary culture. They are also one of the most commonly used utensils in the world. The use of chopsticks can be traced back more than 3,000 years. Chopsticks are not just utensils; they also carry rich meanings. They are used in pairs, with one stick held steady while the other moves, representing the philosophical concept of yin and yang. The length of chopsticks is typically seven *cun* and six *fen* (approximately 7.66 inches), representing the seven emotions and six desires of human beings. They are usually square at the handle and round at the tip, reflecting the traditional concept of "heaven is round and earth is square".

Chopsticks gradually spread to neighboring countries in ancient times and have become dining tools in many countries in East Asia and Southeast Asia. The first person to introduce chopsticks to Europe was Italian missionary Matteo Ricci (1552-1610). Today, many Western families have chopsticks, and in Germany, there is even a "Chopstick Museum" that houses thousands of chopsticks from different historical periods. While representing Eastern culinary culture, using chopsticks is no longer exclusive to the Chinese.

饺子

饺子是一种中国传统面食，以面皮包馅，形如半月形或元宝形，以蒸、煮、煎等方式烹饪。相传饺子是东汉时期“医圣”张仲景发明的，用面皮把祛寒的药材和食材包好并煮熟食用，用于预防和治疗疾病。后来，饺子逐渐演变为中国北方民间的主食和年节食品。人们在春节这个辞旧迎新的时刻吃饺子，寓意“更岁交子”“招财进宝”，祈盼新年吉祥如意。饺子不仅是一种美食，还是一种情结，传达了中国人对美好生活的向往。吃饺子已经成为中国节庆的民俗传统。

Dumplings

Dumplings are a traditional Chinese food made by wrapping filling in dough, shaped like a half-moon or an ingot. They can be cooked by steaming, boiling, or frying. According to legend, they were invented by Zhang Zhongjing, the "medical sage," during the Eastern Han Dynasty (25-220). He used dough to wrap food ingredients and medicinal herbs said to be able to prevent and treat colds and other diseases. Dumplings went on to become a staple dish in northern China and a popular festival food during the Spring Festival. People eat dumplings during the Spring Festival, a time to bid farewell to the old and welcome the new, to symbolize renewal and wealth, hoping for good luck and good fortune in the coming year. Dumplings are more than a delicious food. They also convey the Chinese people's longing for a better life.

八大菜系

八大菜系，是中国饮食文化中具有鲜明地方风味特色，并为社会公认的菜肴流派，包含鲁菜、川菜、粤菜、苏菜、闽菜、浙菜、湘菜、徽菜。由于不同区域气候、地形、历史、物产及饮食风俗的不同，各地膳食文化经过长期演变，形成了自成体系的烹饪技艺和风味菜品，成为中国饮食文化的鲜明标识。

八大菜系各有特色：鲁菜起源于山东的齐鲁风味，口味以咸鲜为主，比较擅长烹饪海鲜；川菜起源于四川、重庆，以麻、辣、鲜、香为特色，善用麻辣调味；粤菜是广东风味的菜肴，口味鲜香，选料精细；苏菜由南京、徐海、淮扬和苏南四种风味组成，用料严谨，造型别致，是中国国宴的主要菜品；闽菜是福建地方菜系，口味以鲜香为主，长于红糟调味、制汤和使用糖醋；浙菜口味以清淡为主，菜式小巧玲珑，菜品鲜美滑嫩；湘菜是湖南的菜肴，讲究热辣、浓鲜，油重色浓；徽菜即安徽菜，口味以咸鲜为主，擅长烧、炖、

Eight major cuisines of China

The eight major cuisines of China refer to China's eight major regional culinary traditions, each with its distinctive local flavors, including Shandong, Sichuan, Cantonese, Jiangsu, Fujian, Zhejiang, Hunan, and Anhui cuisines. Each region has developed its own culinary culture with distinct cooking methods and flavors over time based on its unique climate, geography, history, availability of produce, and dietary customs. Collectively these cuisines represent Chinese food culture.

Each of the eight major cuisines of China has its unique characteristics. Shandong cuisine has distinct salty and fresh flavors and is renowned for its seafood dishes. Sichuan cuisine, originating from Sichuan and Chongqing, is characterized by savory flavors with a spicy or numbing-spicy twist owing to the use of Sichuan pepper. Cantonese cuisine from Guangdong Province emphasizes the quality of ingredients to ensure fresh and savory tastes. Jiangsu cuisine, including four subsets – Nanjing Style, Xuzhou and Haizhou Style, Huai'an and Yangzhou Style, and Suzhou and Nantong Style – is renowned for its careful ingredient selection and plating and is often seen at China's state banquets. Fujian cuisine is famous for its soups and its use of fermented red yeast rice and sweet and sour sauce. Zhejiang cuisine emphasizes light and delicate flavors. It features small and exquisite dishes that are tender and delicious. Hunan cuisine is known for its hot and spicy flavors, fresh aroma and deep colors. Anhui cuisine features salty and fresh flavors, employing cooking techniques such as stewing,

熏、蒸类的功夫菜。

八大菜系根植于中国人“食不厌精、脍不厌细”的传统理念，经过几百年古法传承和技艺创新，奠定了中国菜肴精细、中和、美味、美观、健康的良好基础。这些菜系不仅代表了中国各地区独特的生活饮食风格，更体现了中华民族多元一体的思想文化和群体性格。

smoking, steaming, and braising.

The eight major cuisines of China are rooted in the traditional Chinese belief that there is no limit to fine cooking. Centuries of inter-generational transmission together with innovation in cooking techniques have laid the groundwork for Chinese cuisine to develop delicate, balanced, delicious, visually appealing, and healthy foods. Representing the unique cooking styles of various regions in China, these cuisines embody cohesion in diversity of the Chinese nation.

茶文化

中国是茶叶的故乡，也是茶文化的发源地。上古时期的先人们发现并利用茶，距今已有4700多年历史。人们在产茶、制茶、饮茶等过程中形成了茶文化，包括茶史、茶俗、茶歌、茶礼、茶具、茶艺、茶文学等。

“开门七件事，柴米油盐酱醋茶。”三国两晋时期，民间已有饮茶的习惯，并逐渐传入宫廷，影响到社会上层人士。到了唐代，饮茶之风更盛，茶文化的集大成者陆羽（约733—804）所著述的《茶经》是世界第一部茶文化专著。从唐宋时期煎茶，元代“蒸青散茶”，到明代“炒青”制茶，

Tea culture

China is the birthplace of tea and tea culture. Our ancestors discovered tea more than 4,700 years ago. The cultivation, brewing, and consumption of tea evolved over time to create China's rich tea culture encompassing a diverse range of tea traditions, including tea drinking etiquette; customs, songs, and ceremonies associated with preparing and drinking tea; tea utensils; and tea-inspired art and literature.

An old saying goes: "Firewood, rice, oil, salt, soy sauce, vinegar, and tea are the seven essentials of daily life for ordinary people". Tea drinking became a popular habit among the general population during the Three Kingdoms (220-265), Western Jin (265-316), and Eastern Jin (317-420) dynasties. Eventually, it made its way to the royal court and was embraced by the upper class of society. Tea continued to grow in popularity during the Tang Dynasty (618-907), and the tea connoisseur Lu Yu (c.733-804) wrote the *Classic of Tea*, the world's first monograph on tea culture. Tea processing methods evolved over time, from steaming tea leaves in the Tang and Song dynasties (618-1279) to steaming loose teas in the Yuan Dynasty (1206-1368), and then to roasting and dehydration in the Ming Dynasty (1368-1644). The distinction between black tea and green tea did not come about until the invention

◀ 1 茶杯 teacup
2 茶盏 Chawan (tea bowl)
3 茶壶 tea pot
4 茶则 Chaze tea scoop
5 茶叶 tea leaves

再到清代产生红茶、绿茶之分，茶文化融入社会生活的方方面面，成为人们最喜爱的饮品。

在当代，饮茶和品茶贯穿于中国人的日常生活。人们采取泡、煮等方式，在家庭、工作场所、茶馆、餐厅、寺院等场所饮用茶与分享茶。以茶敬客、以茶敦亲、以茶睦邻、以茶结友，体现了谦、和、礼、敬的价值观，对中国人的道德修养和人格塑造产生了深远影响。

茶起源于中国，盛行于世界。自古以来，茶和茶文化便作为中国对外交流的重要媒介，通过古代丝绸之路和茶马古道等向世界传播，深受各国人民喜爱，在世界文明交流互鉴和人类社会可持续发展中发挥着重要作用。2022年，“中国传统制茶技艺及其相关习俗”列入联合国教科文组织人类非物质文化遗产代表作名录。

of black tea during the Qing Dynasty (1616-1911). Today, tea culture has blended into all aspects of social life and tea has become a beloved drink among the people.

Ubiquitous in everyday life, tea is served steeped or boiled in homes, workplaces, tea houses, restaurants, and temples. The values of modesty, harmony, courtesy, and respect are embodied through sharing tea with guests, relatives, neighbors, and friends, contributing to moral and personality development.

Tea has become popular worldwide. Since ancient times, tea and tea culture have served as important means for China to communicate with the outside world. Thanks to the ancient Silk Road and the Tea Horse Road, tea culture spread around the world and is now appreciated by people of many countries. This has facilitated exchanges and mutual learning between world civilizations, as well as contributing to the development of human society. In 2022, China's traditional tea processing techniques and associated social practices were included in the UNESCO Representative List of Intangible Cultural Heritage of Humanity.

汉服

汉服即“汉民族传统服饰”，是一套包括衣裳、首服、发式、面饰、鞋履、配饰等的整体衣冠系统，浓缩了纺织、蜡染等工艺和美学，传承了30多项中国非物质文化遗产。古代中国又被称为“华夏”，其中“华”字就蕴含了“服饰华美”之意。

相传4000多年前，黄帝发明衣裳，汉服由此起源。此后，汉服经历了复杂的演变过程，服饰种类日渐繁多，纹样和工艺不断丰富，既有百姓的日常穿着，也有君主和百官的正式礼服，构筑出庞大的服制体系。汉服的典型标志是“交领右衽”，左、右两侧衣襟在领口处交叉形成“交领”，在外观上表现为“y”字形，形成整体服饰向右倾斜的效果，体现“以右为尊”的传统观念。汉服的礼服一般是宽袖，多绘有各种纹样，显示出穿戴者的身份特征，成为封建社会等级差别和礼制范式的重要内容。

Hanfu

Hanfu covers a complete set of the traditional attire worn by the Han people, including clothes, headwear, hairstyles, face ornaments, shoes, and accessories. *Hanfu* represents more than 30 traditions of China's intangible cultural heritage. It is an embodiment of the artistry and craftsmanship of textile weaving and dyeing. China was known as *huaxia* in ancient times, in which the character *hua* implies fine attire.

Legend has it that *Hanfu* as a fashion style was developed by Huangdi (the Yellow Emperor) more than 4,000 years ago. It subsequently evolved with the changing times resulting in a plethora of clothing types, patterns, and craftsmanship, including daily wear for the common people and formal attire for monarchs and officials, creating rigid dress codes. The y-shaped *jiaoling* youren is a typical style of *Hanfu*, featuring overlapping collars at the front that close to the right side, reflecting the traditional concept that the right side has priority. Ceremonial Hanfu typically has wide sleeves and is decorated with various patterns that reflect the wearer's identity and status. It developed to fit into feudal society's hierarchy and ceremonial systems.

汉服文化不仅讲究审美，还要符合礼制，生动展现了“衣冠上国”“礼仪之邦”“锦绣中华”的美誉。汉服文化随着古丝绸之路和人员往来而广泛传播，对处于儒家文化圈的朝鲜、日本、韩国、越南等国家产生了深远影响，其款式和纹饰对西方国家服饰文化的发展产生了积极影响。

In addition to a focus on aesthetics, *Hangfu* highlights the importance of ritual conformity, and vividly reflects China's reputation as a nation prizes proper and fine attire, values etiquette, and celebrates splendor and beauty. *Hanfu* spread widely along the ancient Silk Road and through people-to-people exchanges, and left its mark especially on countries under the influence of Confucian culture, such as Korea, Japan, and Vietnam. Its styles and patterns have also found their way into the fashions of the Western world.

旗袍

旗袍，原指清代旗人所穿的长袍和民国女性的改良旗袍，是中国多民族服饰文化融合的产物。20世纪20年代至40年代末，旗袍风行，成为当时最普遍的女子服装。在时代风尚的影响下，旗袍逐渐吸取西式服装的剪裁和结构特点，形成更加国际化和现代化的样式风格。改良后的旗袍让女性的体态美和曲线美得到充分展现，迎合了当时女性解放的思想风潮，因而深受广大女性的喜爱。

旗袍是中国服饰文化的重要标识。近年来，在许多国际场合都能见到中国女性身着旗袍、优雅礼仪的靓丽身影。旗袍传达出的东方审美和文化元素，成为众多国际品牌时尚设计的灵感来源，受到世界各国女性的青睐。

Qipao

The *Qipao* has its origin in the long robes Manchu people wore in the Qing Dynasty (1616-1911). It evolved into the iconic dress in the years after the founding of the Republic of China (1912-1949), as a result of the fusion of China's multi-ethnic fashion styles. From the 1920s to the late 1940s, the *qipao* was in vogue and became the most popular women's garment of the time. As time passed, the design of the *qipao* further evolved and incorporated tailoring details and structural features of Western clothing, making it more international and fashionable. The adapted *qipao* accentuates female beauty and curves. Fitting the context of women's liberation movement of the time, it grew quickly in popularity.

The *qipao* is an important example of Chinese fashion. In recent years, Chinese women have been seen wearing the *qipao* on many international occasions, exhibiting its elegance and beauty. The Eastern aesthetic and cultural elements the *qipao* conveys have become a source of inspiration for some international fashion brands and won the hearts of many across the globe.

丝绸

丝绸是中国优秀传统文化的重要标识。这种用蚕丝或人造丝织造的纺织品，具有光泽柔和、穿着舒适、吸放湿性好等特性。

中国是丝绸的故乡，中国古代劳动人民发明并大规模生产丝绸制品。据考古学发现和推测，在距今五六千年前的新石器时代中期，中国先人们就开始养蚕取丝、纺织丝绸。传说4000多年前，黄帝的妻子嫘祖就发明了“养蚕取丝”的技术。在汉代以前，中国是唯一能生产丝绸的国家，丝绸成为华夏文明的重要标志物。从西汉时期开始，中国丝绸大量运往国外，受到当地人们的广泛欢迎，成为工业革命前国际贸易的主要物资，并由此开启了世界历史上第一次东西方大规模商贸交流，形成中国通往西方的古代丝绸之路，促进了东西方文明交流。

几千年来，中国丝绸产品以其卓越的品质、精美的花

Silk

Silk is an important symbol of traditional Chinese culture. The fabric, which can be made from natural silk or synthetic fibers, boasts distinct features including a soft luster, a comfortable texture, and excellent moisture regain and release properties.

China is the birthplace of silk. The ancient Chinese are credited with bringing this material to the world and putting it into mass production. Based on archaeological discoveries and assumptions, it is believed that the Chinese started to cultivate silkworms and weave silk around 5,000 to 6,000 years ago, during the middle of the Neolithic period. According to legend, Leizu, the wife of Huangdi (the Yellow Emperor), discovered the technique of raising silkworms and weaving silk fabric over 4,000 years ago. China's dominance in silk production technology continued until the Han Dynasty (206 B.C. - A.D. 220), cementing the place of silk as a crucial symbol of Chinese civilization. Export of Chinese silk in large quantities started in the Western Han Dynasty (206 B.C.- A.D. 25) and found receptive consumers throughout the world. Before the Industrial Revolution, silk became a major commodity in international trade, facilitating the emergence of an extensive trade network connecting the East and the West that was the first of its kind. The ancient Silk Road connecting China to the West came into being, which played a huge role in facilitating the exchange of cultures between the East and the West.

For centuries, Chinese silk products have been renowned

色、丰富的文化内涵闻名于世。中国的蚕桑技术、缫丝和丝织提花技术还对西方的纺织技术和近代欧洲纺织工业革命产生了重大的影响，促进了欧洲纺织技术的提升和机械生产的革新。

for their exceptional quality, exquisite colors, and rich cultural connotations. China's sericulture techniques, silk reeling methods and jacquard weaving technology also played a significant role in spurring the modern European textile industry revolution, resulting in technological advances and innovations, especially the use of new machines in textile production.

刺绣

刺绣俗称“绣花”，即用绣针引彩线，在织物上绣成纹样或文字的一种传统手工艺。刺绣随着丝织品的产生与发展逐渐兴起。刺绣针法共有几十种，采用不同的针法会有不同的线条组织和独特的艺术表现效果。

据记载，4000多年前就有在衣裳上绘画和刺绣的做法。在河南发现的商代刺绣实物，是中国现存最早的刺绣工艺品，已经达到相当高的工艺水平。刺绣在宋代达到高峰，宋徽宗（1082—1135）时期将书画艺术融入刺绣工艺之中，形成独特的观赏性刺绣作品。明清时期，随着商业发展，江苏的苏绣、广东的粤绣、湖南的湘绣、四川的蜀绣四大门类广受欢迎，被称为“四大名绣”，其中以苏绣最负盛名。除了四大名绣，中国还有京绣、鲁绣、汴绣等地方名绣，许多少数民族也都有自己特色的民族刺绣。刺绣以针为笔，以线为墨，做工精美，沿传至今，展现着中国古典美学的独特魅力。

Embroidery

Embroidery, also known as "needlework," is a traditional handicraft that involves using a needle and colorful threads to create patterns or characters on fabric. This craft became popular alongside the production and development of silk fabrics. There are many different techniques used in embroidery, with dozens of needlework styles available, each producing its own unique stitching and artistic effects.

Records show that over 4,000 years ago, people were already painting and embroidering on clothing. The earliest surviving examples of Chinese embroidery are from the Shang Dynasty (1600-1046 B.C.) and were discovered in Henan Province; they display a high level of craftsmanship. During the Song Dynasty (960-1279), especially during the reign of Emperor Huizong (1082-1135), embroidery reached its pinnacle when calligraphy and painting were fused with embroidery to create unique ornamental works. The Ming and Qing dynasties (1368-1911) saw the rise of the four famous embroidery styles – Su embroidery from Jiangsu, Yue embroidery from Guangdong, Xiang embroidery from Hunan, and Shu embroidery from Sichuan – which gained in popularity with the development of commerce. Among these, Su embroidery is the best-known. In addition to the four famous embroidery styles, there are also other local styles such as Jing embroidery, Lu embroidery, and Bian embroidery. Additionally, many ethnic minorities have their unique styles of embroidery. Using needles as pens and threads as ink and showcasing the distinctive charm of Chinese classical aesthetics, embroidery displays exquisite workmanship and has been passed down through the centuries.

四合院

四合院是一种中国传统合院式建筑。“四”指东、西、南、北四面，“合”即四面房屋围在一起。早在3000多年前，中国就有完整的四合院出现。根据不同的地理气候条件，各地四合院呈现出不同的形态。其中以北京四合院最为典型。

四合院以家庭为单位建造，通常坐北朝南，庭院方正，空间讲究对称，功能和分区明确。整个院落以“院”为中心，长辈居住正房（北房），有大客厅，晚辈居住厢房。另有客房、厨房、佣人房、贮藏间等，各自独立，起居方便。四合院只开一个大门，通常位于东南侧而非正中，门后设有影壁，用于美化院落、遮挡视线。院内房门都开向院落，促

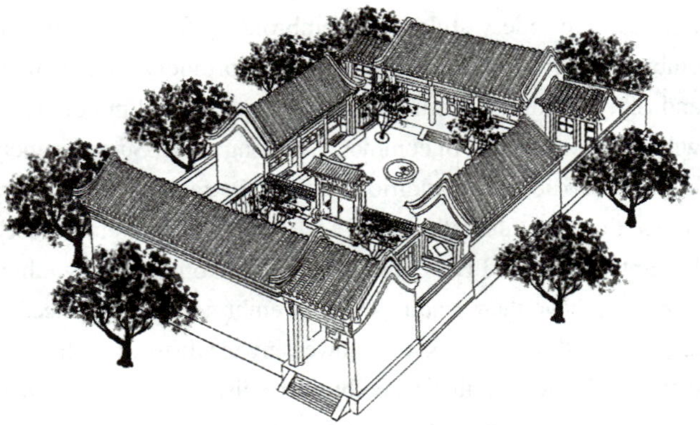

Si He Yuan

Si He Yuan, or courtyard surrounded by buildings on all four sides, is a traditional Chinese style of architecture. Complete versions of *Si He Yuan* have existed in China for over 3,000 years. Due to varying geographical and climatic conditions, *Si He Yuan* display distinct forms in different regions. Beijing's *Si He Yuan* are the best-known example of this architectural style.

A *Si He Yuan* is a family-based dwelling with a square courtyard in the center. It emphasizes symmetry, with clear functions and partitions. It consists of a main house for family elders, which is typically positioned to the north and south-facing with a large living room, and side houses for younger family members. There are also guest rooms, kitchens, servants' quarters, and storage rooms. A *Si He Yuan* typically features only one entrance, which is normally located on the southeast side rather than in the center of the courtyard. A screen wall is often placed behind the entrance for beautification and privacy purposes. The doors of the rooms inside a *Si He Yuan* all face

使一家人和美相亲、其乐融融。庭院内可以植树栽花、饲鸟养鱼、叠石造景，美化生活环境。基于四合院方正合围的基本格局，中国社会逐渐形成了以家庭院落为中心，街坊邻里为干线，社区地域为平面的社会网络系统。

作为居住建筑形态，四合院小可作普通民居，大可作皇宫王府。其营造建筑所讲究的风水学，是中国传统建筑理论的重要组成部分。四合院装修、雕饰、彩绘等体现着传统文化和民间习俗，表达了人们对幸福美好生活的追求。

the courtyard, emphasizing family unity and harmony. The courtyard is often decorated with plants, trees, bird houses, fish tanks, and rock formations, creating a serene and peaceful environment. The idea of the basic layout of the courtyard dwelling has influenced the formation of social networks in China from extended families to neighborhoods to larger communities.

As a residential architectural form, *Si He Yuan* can serve as a simple, ordinary dwelling or a grand palace for royals and nobles. The feng shui principles incorporated into its architecture are a fundamental aspect of traditional Chinese architectural theory. *Si He Yuan* decorations, carving, and painting reflect traditional culture and folk customs, expressing people's pursuit of a happy and beautiful life.

中国园林

中国是世界园林艺术起源最早的国家之一。园林艺术最早可以追溯到3000多年前的殷周时期，人们山水审美观念的确立，促进中国古典园林的产生和发展。

历史上，中国园林伴随着社会文化的发展及人们对理想家园的追求而逐步成熟，形成独具特色的园林体系和异彩纷呈的地域风格。按照地域，中国园林主要分为北方园林、江南园林、岭南园林和蜀中园林等。北方园林主要是皇家园林，规模宏大，建筑庄严，色彩华丽，风格雍容华贵，典型代表有圆明园、颐和园、承德避暑山庄等。江南园林一般面积不大，注重灵活运用造园手法，在小范围内表现大千世界的美景，如苏州留园、拙政园等。岭南园林受西方建筑文化的影响，布局形式和局部构件常采用罗马式的拱形门窗和巴洛克的柱头，比较著名的有顺德清晖园、东莞可园等。蜀中园林风格古朴，常将田园之景移至园内，一些名园大多用于纪念历史名人，如成都杜甫草堂、武侯祠等。

Chinese Gardens

China was one of the first countries to create garden art. The art of gardening can be traced back over 3,000 years to the Yin and Zhou dynasties, during which people's aesthetic conceptualization of mountains and waters promoted the emergence and development of classical gardens in China.

Over the centuries, Chinese gardens have gradually developed their unique characteristics and diverse regional styles, driven by the development of society and culture and people's pursuit of an ideal home. Chinese gardens can be divided on a regional basis into northern, southern, Lingnan, and Sichuan gardens. Northern gardens, mostly royal, are characterized by grand scale, majestic architecture, gorgeous colors, and elegant style, with typical examples including the Old Summer Palace (Yuan Ming Yuan), the Summer Palace, and the Chengde Mountain Resort. Southern gardens, usually smaller in size, emphasize flexible use of gardening techniques to showcase the beauty of the world in a small area, such as the Lingering Garden and the Humble Administrator's Garden in Suzhou. Lingnan gardens, influenced by Western architectural culture, often adopt Roman-style arches and Baroque column heads in their layout and components. Well-known examples include the Qinghui Garden in Shunde and the Keyuan Garden in Dongguan. Sichuan gardens, simple in style, often incorporate pastoral scenery. Some famous gardens commemorate historical celebrities, such as the Du Fu Thatched Cottage and the Wuhou Shrine in Chengdu.

中国园林是中华优秀传统文化的重要组成部分，是具有生命力的文化形态，集中体现了中华民族“道法自然”“天人合一”“兼收并蓄”等哲学思想，彰显了中国传统文化的独特魅力。中国园林以丰富多彩的内容和高超的艺术水平在世界造园艺术中独树一帜，其深厚的文化内涵和辉煌的艺术成就对东西方造园理念和实践产生了广泛影响。

Chinese gardens are an integral part of China's rich traditional culture and a dynamic cultural form that embodies key philosophical concepts such as "the way of nature", "harmony between heaven and humanity", and "inclusiveness and integration". These gardens showcase the unique charm of traditional Chinese culture. With their rich cultural meanings and high level of artistry, Chinese gardens stand out in the world of gardening art and have exerted a wide-ranging influence on gardening ideas and practices in both the East and the West.

中轴线

中轴线是中国传统建筑物（群）中轴对称布局的中心线，是中国传统建筑格局与城市布局的重要特征，源于古代中国人对于天地轴线的理解。中国古代重要建筑大多呈中轴对称格局，主要建筑按照一定的原则分布在中轴线及其两侧，南北层次分明，东西对称分布，布局严谨。

中轴线的建筑格局与“居中”“居北”“面南”的观念有机结合。基于这种理念，中国古代都城大多较为方正。北京中轴线是中轴线建筑格局的集大成者，有外城、内城、皇城、宫城四重城阙，故宫在最中心，形成了独特的城市建筑秩序。北京中轴线南起永定门，经天安门、午门，穿过故宫的太和殿、中和殿、保和殿，越过景山，北至钟鼓楼，全长7.8公里，是北京城的重要标志，也是世界上现存最长的城市中轴线。

中轴线是中国古代都城建筑格局的突出体现。从夏商时

Central Axis

The central axis determines the symmetrical layout of traditional Chinese buildings. An important feature of traditional Chinese architectural and urban layout, it originated from the ancient Chinese understanding of the axis of the heavens and the earth. Most of the important groups of buildings in ancient China had a symmetrical layout along a central axis, with the main buildings constructed along the axis or on its two sides. The buildings follow a rigorous layout, with clearly-divided sections from the north to the south, and symmetrical distribution on the eastern and western sides.

The architectural layout based on the central axis is coupled with the preference for being in the center and facing the south with the back of the building to the north. Because of such preferences, most ancient Chinese capitals were relatively square. The Central Axis of Beijing is the epitome of this architectural layout; it organizes the four layers of the city – the outer city, the inner city, the imperial city, and the imperial palaces, which form a unique urban architectural order. The imperial palaces, also known as the Forbidden City, occupy the very center of the city. The axis is 7.8 kilometers long, starting in the south of the city from the Yongding Gate, running across the Tian'anmen Rostrum, the Meridian Gate, the Forbidden City, and the Jingshan Hill, and ending with the Drum Tower and Bell Tower in the north. It is an important symbol of Beijing and the longest surviving urban central axis in the world.

The central axis is a prominent feature of the architectural

期的偃师、秦汉时期的长安城、汉魏时期的洛阳、隋唐时期的长安，到燕下都、金中都、元大都和明清北京城，再到1949年后的北京城建设，都是以一条轴线为中心对称的格局。中轴线体现了中华文明以中为本、以和为贵的精神，展示了中国人通过规划布局表达对政治理念、文化象征和生活空间的认识发展。

layout of ancient Chinese capitals. The construction of the capital was based on a central axis from the earliest Xia and Shang dynasties all the way to the Ming and Qing dynasties. After the founding of the People's Republic of China in 1949, the construction of Beijing continued to follow this symmetrical layout. The central axis embodies Chinese civilization's emphasis on the doctrine of the mean and the pursuit of harmony, and demonstrates the Chinese understanding of politics, culture, and living spaces.

榫卯结构

榫卯结构是中国传统木构件的一种主要连接方式，它既是中式家具的重要特征，又是传统建筑的主要构件。榫卯，是榫头卯眼的简称，即传统木制家具和古建筑构件接合处的凸凹部分，主要用于连接和固定两个构件。通过榫卯的嵌合，可接长或拼合木料，形成稳固的联结节点以建成所需要的结构和构件，不使用钉子和胶水，就能让木构件之间紧密扣合、严丝合缝、稳定可靠。

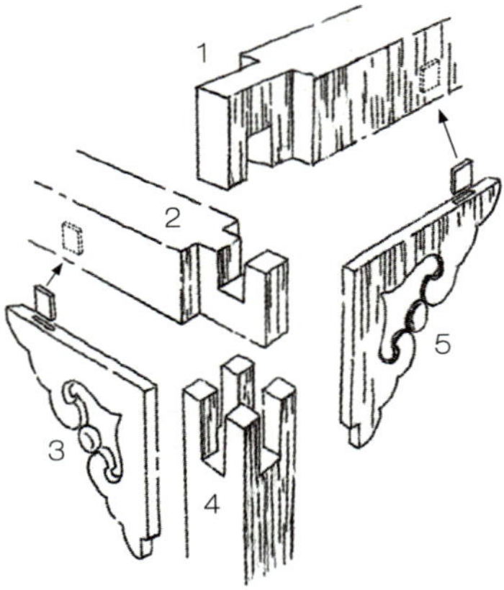

Mortise and Tenon Structure

The mortise and tenon joint is a major traditional method of connecting wooden components in China. It is a vital part of traditional Chinese furniture and architecture. The mortise and tenon respectively refer to the protruding and recessed parts at the joints of traditional wooden furniture and architecture, which are mainly used to connect two components. By joining the mortise and tenon, pieces of wood can be connected to form sturdy joints for any structure or component needed. Without the need for nails or glue, the wooden components are tightly fitted, seamless and stable.

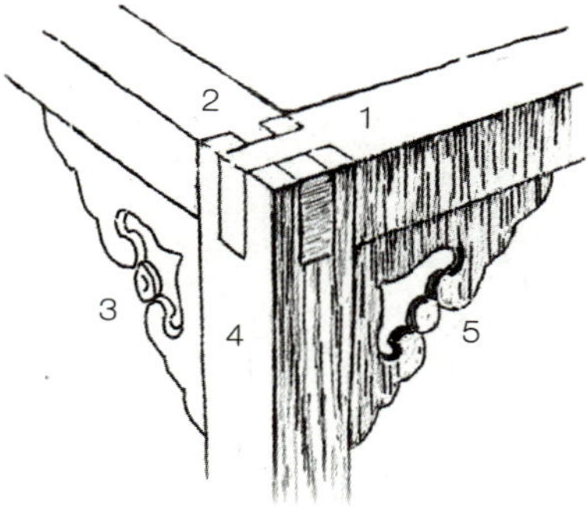

榫卯结构是中国古代匠人的重要发明创造，是中国传统技艺中的优秀代表。北京故宫宫殿、天坛祈年殿、山西悬空寺等传统建筑都将榫卯技艺融入建筑结构之中。榫卯结构“你中有我、我中有你”的凹凸结合连接方式，凝结了中国古代劳动人民的智慧，彰显了中华文明的和合精神。这一技艺至今仍被广泛使用。

The mortise and tenon structure is an important invention of ancient Chinese craftsmen, and an excellent symbol of traditional Chinese craftsmanship. Traditional buildings such as the palaces of the Forbidden City, the Temple of Heaven, and the Suspended Temples in Shanxi province all adopted this structure. With its interlocking protrusions and recesses, the structure embodies ancient China's wisdom and pursuit of harmony. It is still widely used today.

石狮

狮子是中国古代的祥瑞之兽。汉代张骞通西域之后，狮子作为贡品被送到中国内地。由于其形象威武，被认为有辟邪的功能，与狮子相关的绘画和雕塑逐渐出现。石狮就是以石头为材料雕刻狮子形象的建筑装饰物。中国古人认为，石狮可以辟邪镇宅，常将其放置于大门两侧：左侧的雄狮一般都雕成右前爪玩弄绣球，象征威严尊贵；右侧雌狮则雕成左前爪抚摸幼狮，象征子孙绵延。

历史上，石狮往往用于宫殿或帝王陵墓，其艺术形象经历了一个不断发展的过程，在唐代逐渐定型。到了宋代，石狮更广泛地出现在石窟、寺观、祠庙、住宅和园林中。明清时期，石狮进一步走入普通百姓生活，用于民间建筑装饰。石狮被赋予家宅守护者的文化寓意，寄予了中国人期盼平安美好生活的良愿。

Stone Lion

The lion is a symbol of good luck in ancient China. After Zhang Qian's mission to the Western Regions during the Han Dynasty (206 B.C.-A.D. 220), lions were presented as tribute to Central China. Due to their majestic appearance, they were believed to have the power to ward off evil, and paintings of lions and stone lion sculptures gradually emerged. The ancient Chinese believed that stone lions could ward off evil spirits and protect the household, so they were often placed on both sides of the entrance: the male lion on the left side was usually carved with its right front paw playing with a ball, symbolizing dignity and nobility; the female lion on the right side was carved with its left front paw touching a cub, symbolizing the continuity of the family line.

Throughout history, stone lions were commonly placed in palaces or imperial tombs. Their artistic form went through a continuous development process and gradually became fixed during the Tang Dynasty (618-907). In the Song Dynasty (960-1279), stone lions enjoyed even greater popularity, appearing in grottoes, temples, shrines, residences, and gardens. In the Ming and Qing dynasties (1368-1911), they were further incorporated into the daily lives of ordinary people and used as decorative elements in folk architecture. Symbolizing guardians of homes, stone lions embody the desire for a peaceful and prosperous life.

龙凤呈祥

龙和凤是中华民族的两大图腾，被视为中华民族的象征。龙是古代传说的神异动物，融合了多种动物的形象特征，有鳞有角，兴风降雨，被认为是能够祛邪、避灾的灵物。凤是古代传说中的“百鸟之王”，代表美丽吉祥。因此，龙凤呈祥的图腾寓意着高贵、杰出、华丽、祥瑞，表达了人们期盼风调雨顺、万物和合的太平景象。

在中国，“龙凤呈祥”的意象深入人心，其衍生出的“龙飞凤舞”象征夫妻婚姻美好、家庭幸福，在诸多民间艺术形式得以生动呈现。

Dragon and Phoenix in Auspicious Harmony, or *Long Feng Cheng Xiang*

The dragon and the phoenix are two important symbols of Chinese culture and are considered totems of the Chinese nation. The dragon, a mythical creature from ancient Chinese legends, embodies the characteristics of various animals with scales and horns, and is capable of controlling the weather and warding off evil spirits. The dragon is also considered a spiritual being that brings good luck and prosperity. Known as the "queen of one hundred birds", the phoenix represents beauty and auspiciousness in ancient Chinese mythology. Thus, the totem of dragon and phoenix symbolizes nobility, excellence, magnificence, and good fortune, embodying people's aspirations for a tranquil and harmonious world and a prosperous and flourishing future.

In Chinese culture, the image of "龙凤呈祥" (*Long Feng Cheng Xiang*) holds a deep significance in the hearts of people. The derivative expression "龙飞凤舞" (*Long Fei Feng Wu*, the dance of dragons and phoenixes) has become a symbol of marital bliss and happy family life, and is vividly depicted in various forms of folk art.

十二生肖

十二生肖又名“十二属相”，是用于纪年的12种动物，包括鼠、牛、虎、兔、龙、蛇、马、羊、猴、鸡、狗、猪。中国古人将十二生肖与纪年的十二地支相配，组成子鼠、丑牛、寅虎、卯兔、辰龙、巳蛇、午马、未羊、申猴、酉鸡、戌狗、亥猪，以十二年为一个周期，形成一种传统的纪年法。人的出生年份与当年的生肖相对应，如卯年生的人属兔，申年生的人属猴等。

十二生肖是历史悠久、代代相传的民俗文化符号。在中国，人们知道自己和亲人的生肖，民间也有许多关于十二生肖的有趣故事和传说，特别是在春节，十二生肖作为吉祥物，广泛呈现在春联、剪纸、邮票、绘画、雕塑等艺术领域，寄托中国人对美好生活的祝福与期盼。

The Chinese Zodiac

The Chinese zodiac assigns an animal to each year in a repeating 12-year cycle. The 12 animals are rat, ox, tiger, rabbit, dragon, snake, horse, sheep, monkey, rooster, dog, and pig. The ancient Chinese paired the 12 animals with the 12 earthly branches, forming a traditional system of ordinals with a 12-year cycle. A person's zodiac sign is thus determined by the year of their birth. For example, those born in the year of Mao will have the zodiac sign of the rabbit. Those born in the year of Shen will have the zodiac sign of the monkey.

The Chinese zodiac, a symbol of Chinese folk culture passed down from generation to generation, enjoys a long history. In China, people identify themselves and their families with zodiac animals. There are many intriguing stories and legends about them. The animals are often presented as auspicious signs, especially during the Spring Festival. They appear on spring couplets, paper-cuttings, stamps, paintings, sculptures, and other art works, representing the Chinese people's wishes and hopes for a happy life.

春节

春节即中国农历新年，是中华民族最隆重的传统节日，承载着除旧布新、拜神祭祖、祈福辟邪、亲朋团圆、欢庆娱乐等功能。春节历史悠久，起源于中国远古时期人们的原始信仰和自然崇拜，由祭祀祈年活动演变而来。中国古人认为，春回大地、万象更新，春天开启新的年岁轮回，这在农耕社会具有重要意义。今天，人们把农历正月初一定为春节，节庆活动一直延续到农历正月十五。

年画
Nianhua (Spring Festival picture)

Spring Festival

The Spring Festival, also known as the Chinese Lunar New Year, is the most important traditional festival of the Chinese nation. During the festival, people cast out the old and usher in the new. They worship gods and ancestors, pray for good fortune, and gather with family and friends for celebrations. The Spring Festival has a long history. Originating in primitive beliefs and the worship of nature in ancient China, it evolved from the practices of offering sacrifices and praying for good harvests. The ancient Chinese believed that spring is the time when everything rejuvenates and a new year begins. A good start to a new year was of great significance in an agrarian society. Today as before, people celebrate the first day of the first lunar month as the Spring Festival with festive activities, which continue until the 15th of the month.

门神
Menshen (guardians of doors and gates)

阖家团圆、共聚一堂，是春节的重要内涵。在春节将近时，家家户户都在大门两边贴上崭新的春联，以上联、下联、横批的独特文学形式，表达人们对新一年的美好愿望。人们还在屋门、墙壁、门楣等处贴上象征好运的“福”字，张贴驱邪魔、保平安的年画和门神，并在庭院或房屋门口挂起大红灯笼，烘托隆重热烈的节庆气氛，寄托对幸福生活的期待。春节的前一天即除夕，家家户户团聚享用丰盛的年夜饭。春节期间，人们要穿上新衣，走亲访友，问候拜年，彼此表达美好祝愿。燃放爆竹、舞龙舞狮也是春节的节庆习俗，用来祈求风调雨顺、事事如意。到了正月十五元宵节，人们还会吃元宵，举行游艺活动，完成春节的迎春仪式。

春节是中华传统文化的重要组成部分，承载着博大精深的中华文化底蕴，展现着中国人丰富多彩的社会文化生活。当前，春节已经走进全球近200个国家，世界各地的春节年味越来越浓。春节以欢乐祥和的气氛和独特的文化魅力，逐渐成为世界人民共同的节日。

Family reunions are the most important part of the Spring Festival. As the festival approaches, every household posts a new spring couplet on the sides of their door. The couplet, a unique literary form consisting of an upper line (on the right side), a lower line (on the left side), and a horizontal scroll, expresses people's good wishes for the new year. People also post the Chinese character "Fu" (good fortune), Nianhua (Spring Festival picture) and Menshen (guardians of doors and gates) on their doors, walls, and lintels, and hang red lanterns in the courtyard or at the door, to create a festive atmosphere and express their desire for a happy life. On the eve of the Spring Festival, families will have a grand reunion dinner. During the festival, people wear new clothes, visit relatives and friends, and exchange greetings and good wishes. Setting off firecrackers and performing dragon and lion dances are also traditional customs to pray for harvests and good luck. On the 15th of the first lunar month (Lantern Festival), people eat glutinous rice balls and participate in various activities to complete the celebrations of the Spring Festival.

As an important Chinese tradition, celebrating the Spring Festival carries profound cultural meanings and showcases the Chinese people's rich and colorful social and cultural life. With its joyful atmosphere and unique cultural charm, the festival is now celebrated in almost 200 countries and is gaining popularity worldwide as a happy event shared by all.

元宵节

农历正月十五是中国传统节日元宵节。“元宵”意为一年中第一个月圆之夜。据道教“三元”的说法，又被称为“上元节”。

西汉时期就已重视正月十五的节庆，东汉明帝为弘扬佛法，下令正月十五夜晚在皇宫和寺庙里点灯敬佛，此后逐渐形成元宵张灯的习俗。隋唐以来，元宵节灯市热闹非凡，灯火如昼，人们出游赏花灯、猜灯谜。从宋代开始，正月十五形成吃元宵或汤圆的传统，“北方‘滚’元宵、南方‘包’

Yuanxiao Festival (Lantern Festival)

China's traditional festival — *Yuanxiao* (Lantern Festival) falls on the fifteenth day of the first month on the Chinese lunar calendar. *Yuanxiao* means the first full moon in a year. Taoism worships *Sanyuan* (Three Primes), with Lantern Festival being the birthdate of the first Prime, the festival is also called *Shangyuan* Festival.

Yuanxiao already received much attention back in the Western Han Dynasty (206 B.C.-A.D. 25). To promote Buddhism, Emperor Mingdi of the Eastern Han Dynasty (25-220) ordered to light up the royal palace and temples to pay tribute to Buddha, which gave birth to the later custom of lighting up lanterns on this day. Since the Sui (581-618) and the Tang (618-907) dynasties, lantern fairs would be held on the night of *Yuanxiao*; on these occasions, bright lanterns would light up the night as if it were daytime, and the lively fairs would hum with people who came to enjoy various-shaped lanterns, and solve riddles on the lanterns. In the Song Dynasty (960-1279), people developed the tradition of eating *yuanxiao* or *tangyuan* (sweet glutinous rice balls) on the Lantern Festival — though of similar nature, the food's name is different due to different making process. People from northern China would make *yuanxiao* by rolling the rice flour with fillings into balls, while those from southern China would use the wrapping method to make *tangyuan*. Both *yuanxiao* and *tangyuan* contains the Chinese character *yuan*, which is a part of the Chinese word *tuanyuan*, meaning getting together with family. In the food re-

汤圆”都有“团圆”之意，象征全家人和睦幸福。

受中华文化影响，韩国、日本、朝鲜、越南等国也有过元宵节的传统，海外华人聚居区也多在元宵节举办各种庆祝活动。

sides people's wish for their family's harmony and happiness.

Influenced by Chinese culture, countries like South Korea, Japan, North Korea and Vietnam all share this traditional festival. In the regions where oversea Chinese communities inhabit, people will hold various activities to celebrate this festival.

清明节

清明节在公历4月5日前后，是二十四节气中的第五个节气，也是中国传统节日，以扫墓祭祖和踏青郊游为主要礼俗主题，兼具自然与人文内涵。

清明节源自上古时期的祖先信仰和春祭习俗，逐渐形成内涵丰富的清明节礼俗，包括扫墓祭祖、郊游踏青、禁火冷食等。按照传统习俗，人们在清明节携带酒食果品、纸钱等物品来到已故亲人的墓地，供祭食物、烧掉纸钱，为墓地培上新土、插上嫩柳，并叩头行礼祭拜。清明节自古传承、延续至今，是中华民族最隆重的祭祖大节，体现了中华民族礼敬祖先、慎终追远的文化传统，成为维系和促进中华儿女情感交流的重要纽带。

Qingming Festival

Qingming Festival usually falls on April the 5th every year. Besides being a traditional festival in China, it is also the fifth one (Qingming, or Clear and Bright) of the 24 solar terms. Rituals and customs on the day of *Qingming* centered around tomb sweeping, paying tribute to ancestors and outings, which reflect Chinese people's perception of nature and life.

Ancestor worship and spring sacrificial ceremonies in prehistory times gave birth to the *Qingming* Festival, and over time, *Qingming* customs have grown richer, including tomb sweeping and ancestor worshiping, spring outings, forbidding fire and eating cold foods, etc. Traditionally, people will bring sacrifices such as drinks, food and joss papers (spirit monies) to the grave of their deceased relatives, offer the food, burn the joss papers, earth up the tomb, stick young willow branches on the graveyard, and kowtow to pay tribute to their ancestors. *Qingming*, as the most significant ancestor-worship festival for the Chinese people, is an important cultural inheritance. It embodies the Chinese people's respect for the ancestors and their solemn attitudes toward death, as part of China's cultural traditions. All these function as a way of the emotional communication of the Chinese people.

端午节

农历五月初五是中国传统节日端午节，是拜神祭祖、祈福辟邪、欢庆娱乐和饮食的民俗大节。

端午节源于中国古人对自然天象的崇拜，由上古时期“祭龙”习俗演变而来，龙和龙舟文化贯穿端午节的历史传承。赛龙舟、吃粽子是端午节最重要的习俗，此外，还有采草药、挂艾草、饮雄黄酒、拴五色丝线、佩香囊等习俗，以期辟邪除灾、祈福纳祥。

端午节是流传于汉字文化圈和华人华侨中的传统节日，而龙舟赛事在欧美地区也颇具影响力。2009年，“端午节”列入联合国教科文组织人类非物质文化遗产代表作名录。

Duanwu Festival (Dragon Boat Festival)

China's traditional festival *Duanwu* falls on the fifth day of the fifth month on the Chinese lunar calendar. It is a major folk festival featuring deity worshiping, ancestor commemoration, praying for happiness, exorcising evil spirits, celebration, entertainment, and gourmet food.

Ancient Chinese's worship of nature and celestial motions have cradled the Dragon Boat Festival, and the customs of the festival derived from "offering sacrifices to the dragon" in prehistory times, which is why dragon and dragon boats have always been the icons for the festival. Besides the most important customs — dragon boat races and eating *Zongzi* (Chinese rice dumplings), there are also other customs like picking herbs, hanging wormwood, drinking *xionghuang* (realgar) wine, wearing five-colored silk threads and sachets and so on, which are gestures to help expel evil spirits and pray for happiness.

Duanwu Festival (Dragon Boat Festival) is celebrated in the Sinographic Sphere and by all those of Chinese nation, home and abroad. Dragon boat races are also influential in European countries and the U.S. In 2009, the Dragon Boat Festival was selected into the UNESCO Representative List of the Intangible Cultural Heritage of Humanity.

中秋节

农历八月十五是中国传统节日中秋节，是赏月颂月、寄托思念、祈盼丰收的传统佳节。

中秋节源于中国古人对月亮等自然天象的崇拜，由上古时期“秋分祭月”传统演变而来。汉代已经有“中秋”的说法，晋代出现中秋赏月的记载。到了唐代，中秋赏月风俗日渐兴盛，人们把中秋与嫦娥奔月、吴刚伐桂、玉兔捣药等神话故事结合起来，许多诗人还留下咏月的著名诗句。北宋时期，农历八月十五被正式定为中秋节，并开始出现中秋节令食品。明清时期，每逢中秋节，人们会在家中摆上圆形果饼作为贡品，向月亮祭拜。如今，祭月拜月活动已演变为规模盛大、多姿多彩的民间赏月游乐活动，吃月饼也已成为中秋节的习俗，被赋予团圆、美满的象征意义。此外，中秋节还

Zhongqiu Festival (The Mid-Autumn Festival)

The Mid-Autumn Festival is celebrated on the fifteenth day of the eighth month on the Chinese lunar calendar. It is a traditional festival for watching and admiring the moon, expressing longing for loved ones and praying for harvests.

The Mid-Autumn Festival could date back to people's initial worship of celestial bodies like the moon, and it derived from the custom of worshiping the moon at the autumn equinox (Sept. 22 or 23) in prehistory times. The word *Zhongqiu*, which literally means "mid-autumn," was already used in the Han Dynasty (206 B.C.-A.D. 220). Historical records show that moon-watching has become an activity for the festival in the Jin Dynasty (265-420). In the Tang Dynasty (618-907), the custom prevailed, and people connected the festival with legends like Chang'e flying to the moon, Wu Gang cutting down the osmanthus tree and the jade rabbit mashing herbs. Many poets also left famous lines about the moon. In the Northern Song Dynasty (960-1127), the fifteenth day of the eighth month on the Chinese lunar calendar was officially set as the Mid-Autumn Festival, and typical food for the festival began to appear. In Ming (1368-1644) and Qing (1616-1911) dynasties, people would place round-shaped fruits and pastries as offerings on the Mid-Autumn Day to pay tribute to the moon.

Nowadays, those rituals have gradually turned into grand and various folk activities where people admire the moon and have fun. Eating mooncakes has also become an indispensable part of the festival, as the mooncakes represent family gather-

有赏桂花、饮桂花酒、吃螃蟹、玩兔儿爷等习俗。中秋节是全世界华人华侨共同的节日。受中华文化影响，东亚和东南亚一些国家也形成了过中秋节的习俗。

ing and happiness. In addition, there are customs like admiring osmanthus flowers, drinking osmanthus flower wine, eating crabs and playing *Tu'er Ye* (figurines of the Rabbit God). The Mid-Autumn Festival is celebrated by all Chinese in the world. Influenced by Chinese culture, some countries in East and Southeast Asia also celebrate the festival.

自然风光与物质文化遗产

Natural Landscape and Tangible Cultural Heritage

基于漫长复杂的地质运动，在中国广袤国土上，众多山脉巍峨耸立，平原沃野千里，大江大河奔腾不息。这些壮阔的自然风光，被赋予丰富的人文内涵，铭刻进中国人的精神世界。中国人用自己的辛勤劳动、聪明才智和团结奋斗，在农耕时代的技术条件下修筑了大量公共工程和宏伟建筑，创造出令世界叹为观止的物质文化遗产，为中华文明绵延千年作出重要贡献。

China is a vast land of natural beauty – resulting from complex geological processes over time – from sweeping plains to towering mountains to mighty rivers. These natural wonders hold significant cultural meaning and have been deeply ingrained in the Chinese psyche. We also congratulate ourselves on benefiting from the abundance of tangible cultural heritage, which our ancestors in what was still an agrarian society created through hard work, ingenuity, and collaborative efforts in the form of numerous public engineering projects and magnificent structures, stunning to the world. These creations have contributed significantly to the continuous development of Chinese civilization over the past thousands of years.

黄河

黄河是中国北方地区的大河，中国第二长河，干流全长5464千米。黄河发源于青藏高原巴颜喀拉山，流经青藏高原、黄土高原和华北平原，最后注入渤海。因中段流经黄土高原地区夹带大量泥沙而呈黄色河水，故称“黄河”。

黄河文化是中华文明的重要组成部分，是中华民族的根和魂。黄河流域是中华文明的主要发源地之一，分布有蓝田文化、半坡文化、龙山文化等大量新石器文化遗址。早在6000多年前，黄河流域内已开始出现农业活动，4000多年前开始形成氏族部落，以炎帝、黄帝两大部族最为强大，后融合其他部族，形成中华民族的前身“华夏族”。中华民族5000多年文明史上，黄河流域有3000多年处于古代中国政治、经济、文化、科技中心，分布有郑州、西安、洛阳、开封、安阳等古都，富集着大量历史遗产和文化景观，黄河也因此成为连通东西国土、沟通欧亚大陆的文化运河，至今仍

The Yellow River

The Yellow River is a major river in northern China and the second-longest river in the country with a total length of 5,464 kilometers. It originates from the Bayan Har Mountains on the Qinghai-Tibet Plateau, flows through the Qinghai-Tibet Plateau, the Loess Plateau, and the North China Plain, and finally empties into the Bohai Sea. The river's name derives from the yellowish color of its water caused by the massive amount of sediment carried from the Loess Plateau in its middle reaches.

The Yellow River is a crucial element of Chinese civilization and the foundation of the Chinese nation. The Yellow River basin is one of the main cradles of Chinese civilization, containing numerous Neolithic cultural sites, such as Lantian, Banpo, and Longshan. Over 6,000 years ago, agriculture began in the Yellow River basin, and clans and tribes began to form over 4,000 years ago, with the tribes led by Yandi Emperor and Yellow Emperor being the most dominant. They later merged with other tribes to form the "*Huaxia* tribe", which was the precursor to the Chinese nation.

For over 3,000 years of China's 5,000-year civilization, the Yellow River basin was the epicenter of ancient China's politics, economy, culture, and technology. It was home to ancient capitals such as Zhengzhou, Xi'an, Luoyang, Kaifeng, and Anyang and is abundant in historical heritage and cultural landscapes. Thus, the Yellow River has become a cultural conduit that connects the east and west of China and the rest of the

然处于重要地位。黄河流域依托农耕文明诞育了地域性传统文化，推动了文学艺术、天文立法、科技建筑、语言习俗等跨文化交流与融合，铸就了中华民族多元一体的根基。黄河也因此被誉为中华民族的“母亲河”。

历史上，黄河水患严重，曾给人民生产生活造成了巨大困扰。从1946年中共领导成立冀鲁豫解放区黄河水利委员会，到中华人民共和国成立70多年来的艰辛探索和不懈努力，黄河治理保护工作取得重大成就，创造了伏秋大汛岁岁安澜的奇迹。

Eurasian continent. It continues to hold a significant position even today.

Agrarian development in the Yellow River basin nurtured regional cultural traditions and promoted cross-cultural exchanges and integration in areas such as literature, art, astronomy, law, technology, architecture, language, and customs. This laid the groundwork for the multi-ethnic integration of the Chinese nation. As a result, the Yellow River is also known as the "Mother River" of the Chinese nation.

Historically, the Yellow River often caused significant damage. Severe flooding occurred from time to time, affecting people's lives and livelihoods. In response, the Communist Party of China established the Yellow River Conservancy Commission for Hebei-Shandong-Henan Liberation Area in 1946. Unrelenting efforts to tame flooding have continued over the past 70 years since the founding of the People's Republic of China, and significant progress has been made in managing and protecting the Yellow River, successfully preventing severe flooding from occurring during flood seasons.

长江

长江是中国第一大河、世界第三长河，位于中国南方，流域面积约占中国陆地总面积的1/5，干流全长近6400千米。长江发源于青藏高原唐古拉山，干流先后流经青藏高原、横断山区、云贵高原、四川盆地、长江中下游平原，最后注入东海。干流通航里程达2800多千米，被称为“黄金水道”。长江水系发达，大小支流2200多条，形成的湖泊总面积约占中国湖泊总面积的1/5。

长江流域是中华文明的主要发源地之一，分布有大溪文化、石家河文化、河姆渡文化、良渚文化等大量新石器文化遗址。长江中游地区是公认的人类稻作文明的发祥地。自春秋时期开始，长江流域的巴蜀文化、荆楚文化、吴越文化迅速发展，特别是荆楚文化可以与黄河流域的中原文化并驾齐驱。唐代中期以后，中国的经济、文化重心逐步南移，长江流域在农业、手工业、文化、艺术、人才教育等诸多方面逐渐超越黄河流域，为中华文明绵延发展作出重要贡献。随着

The Yangtze River

The Yangtze River is the longest river in China and the third-longest in the world. Its mainstem spans nearly 6,400 kilometers. Its drainage basin, covering approximately one-fifth of China's total land area, flows through the southern part of the country. Originating from the Tanggula Mountains on the Qinghai-Tibet Plateau, the river flows through the Qinghai-Tibet Plateau, the Hengduan Mountains, the Yunnan-Guizhou Plateau, the Sichuan Basin, and the Yangtze Plain before eventually emptying into the East China Sea. The river's mainstem is navigable for over 2,800 kilometers, earning it the name "golden waterway". With over 2,200 tributaries, the river system is elaborate, and the total area of its lakes accounts for about one-fifth of China's total lake area.

The Yangtze River basin is considered one of the cradles of Chinese civilization, home to numerous Neolithic cultural sites such as Daxi, Shijiahe, Hemudu, and Liangzhu. The middle reaches of the Yangtze River are considered the birthplace of rice cultivation. Starting from the Spring and Autumn period (770-476 B.C.), Bashu, Jingchu, and Wuyue in the Yangtze River basin witnessed accelerated human flourishing, with Jingchu being on par with the Central Plains in the Yellow River basin. After the mid-Tang Dynasty (618-907), China's economic and cultural center gradually shifted southward, and the Yangtze River basin gradually surpassed the Yellow River basin in many aspects, including agriculture, handicrafts, culture, art, talent cultivation, making significant contributions

海上丝绸之路的兴起，长江流域在中外文化交流和贸易往来方面的作用日益重要，时至今日仍然是中国对外开放的重要前沿阵地。

to the development of Chinese civilization. With the rise of the Maritime Silk Road, the Yangtze River basin played an increasingly important role in cultural exchanges and trade with foreign countries. It continues to be at the forefront of China's opening-up to the outside world.

泰山

中国名山泰山古称岱宗，位于山东省境内，东西长约200千米，南北宽约50千米，主峰玉皇顶海拔1532.7米。泰山山体高大、山势陡峻，蕴藏着奇、险、秀、幽、奥、旷等自然景观特点，被誉为“五岳独尊”。

泰山在中华文明史上占有重要地位，具有丰厚的地理、历史、文化内涵。泰山东望大海，西靠黄河，拥有“云海玉盘”“旭日东升”“晚霞夕照”“黄河金带”等诸多自然奇观。在历史上，泰山因其巍峨挺拔、传说能直通天庭而备受推崇，历代君主在此祭天封禅，祈求国泰民安、江山永固。在文化上，泰山儒、道、佛三教并存，保留寺庙、宫观等建筑群约30处，古遗迹100多处，古代文人墨客如孔子、司马迁、李白、杜甫等都曾登临泰山，留下众多诗文名篇。

Mount Taishan

Mount Taishan, also known as *Daizong* in ancient times, is a renowned mountain located in China's Shandong Province. It stretches approximately 200 kilometers from east to west and 50 kilometers from north to south, with its highest peak, Jade Emperor Peak, reaching an altitude of 1,532.7 meters. Mount Taishan is characterized by its towering cliffs, scenic vistas, secluded valleys, and vast expanses, earning it the title of the "Greatest of the Five Sacred Mountains".

Mount Taishan holds a significant place in the history of Chinese civilization and boasts rich geographical, historical, and cultural connotations. Located between the Yellow River to the west and the East China Sea to the east, it features numerous spots where visitors can have a gorgeous view of a sea of clouds, the sunrise, sunset glows, and a golden belt of the Yellow River. Historically, Mount Taishan was revered for its majestic and legendary power to lead straight to heaven, and emperors of successive dynasties performed worship and sacrificial rituals here to pray for prosperity, peace, and stability. Culturally, Mount Taishan enjoyed the coexistence of Confucianism, Daoism, and Buddhism. There are around 30 temples and palaces and over 100 ancient sites. The mountain was a favorite destination among ancient scholars and poets, such as

1987年，泰山列入联合国教科文组织世界文化与自然遗产名录。2006年，泰山被联合国教科文组织评为世界地质公园。

Confucius, Sima Qian, Li Bai, and Du Fu, who wrote memorable literary pieces at the top of the mountain. In 1987, Mount Taishan was included on the UNESCO World Heritage List as a cultural and natural site, and in 2006, it was designated as a UNESCO Global Geopark.

黄山

中国名山黄山古称黟山，位于安徽省南部，南北长约40千米，东西宽约30千米。黄山境内有千米以上高峰88座，其中莲花峰、光明顶、天都峰为三大主峰，海拔均超过1800米。黄山以奇松、怪石、云海、温泉、冬雪著称于世，被誉为“天下第一奇山”，其中最著名的是黄山迎客松，展现着东方礼仪文化。

黄山拥有丰富的自然景观和人文景观，境内森林覆盖率达84.7%，富集着古蹬道、古楹联、古桥、古亭、古寺、古塔等文化遗存，享有“五岳归来不看山，黄山归来不看岳”的美誉。中国历代文人雅士热衷于游历黄山，以黄山为灵感来源，留下众多摩崖石刻和文学书画作品。1990年，黄山列入联合国教科文组织世界文化与自然遗产名录。2004年，黄山被联合国教科文组织公布为世界地质公园。

Mount Huangshan

Mount Huangshan, also known as Yishan in ancient times, is a famous mountain range located in the southern part of Anhui Province. It spans about 40 kilometers from north to south and 30 kilometers from east to west, with 88 peaks over 1,000 meters high, including the Lotus Peak, the Bright Summit, and the Tiandu Peak, all with an altitude exceeding 1,800 meters. Mount Huangshan is renowned for its unique pine trees, peculiar rocks, sea of clouds, hot springs, and winter snow, earning it the reputation as the "No.1 fantastic mountain in the world". Its most famous attraction is the Welcome Pine, which represents hospitality in Eastern culture.

Mount Huangshan boasts a rich blend of natural beauty and cultural significance, with forest coverage reaching 84.7% and an abundance of cultural elements such as ancient trails, couplets, bridges, pavilions, temples, and pagodas. As an ancient saying goes, "Once you have visited the five sacred mountains of China, there is no need to visit any other mountain; and once you have seen Mount Huangshan, there is no need to see any of the other four sacred mountains". This highlights the unparalleled beauty of Mount Huangshan. Men of letters and artists used to be drawn to the mountain to find inspiration to create original works of calligraphy, painting, and poetry In 1990, Mount Huangshan was included on the UNESCO World Heritage List as a cultural and natural site, and in 2004, it was declared as a UNESCO Global Geopark.

大运河

大运河是中国古代开凿的人工运河，始建于公元前5世纪的春秋时期，至今已有2500多年的历史。大运河纵贯中国东部华北平原和长江中下游平原，包括隋唐大运河、京杭大运河和浙东大运河三部分，全长3000多千米，地跨8个省级行政区，沟通了海河、黄河、淮河、长江、钱塘江五大水系，是中国古代南北交通的大动脉。

大运河是为确保粮食运输安全、维护政权稳定和国家统一，由国家投资开凿和管理的巨大运河工程体系，也是解决中国南北社会和自然资源不平衡的重要措施，实现了在广大国土范围内南北方物资的大跨度调配，沟通了国家的政治中心与经济中心，促进了不同地域间的经济、文化交流，在国家安全、政治稳定、经济繁荣、社会发展、文化交流等方面发挥了不可替代的作用。

大运河是与长城相媲美的中国古代伟大工程，是中国古代劳动人民创造的一项伟大的水利建筑，是世界上最长的运河，也是世界上开凿最早、规模最大的运河。2014年，大运河列入联合国教科文组织世界文化遗产名录。

The Grand Canal

The Grand Canal is an ancient man-made waterway that dates back to the 5th century B.C. during China's Spring and Autumn period. With a history spanning over 2500 years, it traverses the North China Plain and the Yangtze Plain, encompassing three sections: the Sui and Tang Grand Canal, the Beijing-Hangzhou Grand Canal, and the Eastern Zhejiang Canal. Stretching over 3000 kilometers, it passes through eight provincial-level regions and connects the five major river systems, namely the Haihe River, the Yellow River, the Huaihe River, the Yangtze River, and the Qiantang River. The canal served as a major artery of transportation between the north and south in ancient China.

The Grand Canal was a massive engineering project built and managed by the state, aimed at ensuring safe transportation of grain and maintaining political stability and national unity. It was also intended to address natural resource imbalances between northern and southern China and development needs, by facilitating large-scale distribution of goods across the country and connecting the political and economic centers. The canal facilitated economic and cultural exchanges between different regions and played an irreplaceable role in ensuring national security, political stability, economic prosperity, and social development.

One of the greatest engineering marvels of ancient China, comparable to the Great Wall, and a magnificent project of water conservancy, the Grand Canal holds the record for being the longest canal in the world as well as the earliest and largest one ever excavated. In 2014, the Grand Canal was included on the UNESCO World Heritage List.

都江堰

都江堰建于公元前3世纪，位于成都平原西部的岷江，是战国时期秦国蜀郡太守李冰及其子率众修建的一项大型水利工程，也是世界上年代最久、唯一留存、以无坝引水为特征的宏大水利工程，列入世界文化遗产名录、世界自然遗产名录、世界灌溉工程遗产名录。

都江堰水利工程是天人合一、人水和谐的典范，实现了人、地、水三者高度协和统一。都江堰充分利用当地西北高、东南低的地理条件，根据江河出山口处特殊的地形、水脉、水势，乘势利导，无坝引水，自流灌溉，使堤防、分水、泄洪、排沙、控流相互依存，共为体系，保证了防洪、灌溉、水运和社会用水综合效益的充分发挥。都江堰建堰2200多年来经久不衰，让成都平原变为润泽、富足的“天府之国”。德国地理学家李希霍芬曾称赞都江堰完善的灌溉方法无与伦比。

Dujiangyan Irrigation System

The Dujiangyan Irrigation System, situated on the Minjiang River in Sichuan Province, west of the Chengdu Plain, was constructed during the Warring States period (475-221 B.C.) under the direction of Li Bing, governor of Shu in the State of Qin, together with his son. It is the world's oldest and only functioning water conservation project that uses a unique method of diverting water without constructing a dam. It has been included on the UNESCO World Cultural and Natural Heritage List and the International Commission on Irrigation and Drainage (ICID)'s list of World Heritage Irrigation Structures.

The Dujiangyan Irrigation System is a remarkable example of how harmonious human-nature interactions play out when it comes to conservation and management of land and water to benefit humanity. It takes full advantage of the unique geographical conditions of the area where terrain is higher in the northwest and lower in the southeast. Rather than constructing a dam, the system relies on the river's natural flow and distributes the water based on the specific topography at the mountain outlet of the river, as well as water circulation and water veins. The embankments, diversion channels, flood discharge outlets, sediment control, and flow regulation are interdependent, functioning together as a cohesive whole that provides protection against flooding and facilitates irrigation, water transportation, and general water use. The Chengdu Plain owes a great deal to the Dujiangyan Irrigation System for being the "Land of Abundance" for over 2,200 years. German geologist Baron Ferdinand von Richthofen once praised the Dujiangyan Irrigation System as unparalleled.

丝绸之路

丝绸之路，一般指陆上丝绸之路。1877年，德国地质地理学家李希霍芬在《中国》一书中把中国与中亚、中国与印度间以丝绸贸易为媒介的这条西域交通道路命名为“丝绸之路”，这一概念由此广泛传播。

古代丝绸之路起源于汉武帝派张骞（约前164—前114）出使西域所开辟的通道。它以西安为起点，经甘肃、新疆，再经阿富汗、伊朗、伊拉克、叙利亚等而达地中海，以罗马为终点，成为连接亚欧大陆的古代东西方文明的交汇之路。数千年来，人们沿着丝绸之路进行商品、宗教、政治、文化等方面的广泛交流，对东西方文明进步产生深远影响。此外，还有从广州、泉州、杭州、扬州等沿海城市出发，从南洋到阿拉伯海，甚至远达非洲东海岸的海上贸易的“海上丝绸之路”。

古代丝绸之路是一条贸易之路，更是一条友谊之路。在中华民族同其他民族的友好交往中，逐步形成了以和平合作、开放包容、互学互鉴、互利共赢为特征的丝绸之路精神。2013年，中国提出共建“一带一路”重大倡议，赋予

Silk Road

The Silk Road generally refers to an overland route for silk trade, which connected China with Central Asia and India. In 1877, German geographer Ferdinand von Richthofen named this route the "Silk Road" in his book *China: The Results of My Travels and the Studies Based Thereon*, and the concept has since been popularized.

The ancient Silk Road originated from a route opened up by Zhang Qian (around 164-114BC) who was sent by Emperor Wudi of the Western Han Dynasty (206B.C.-A.D.25) to the western regions. It started from Xi'an, passed through Gansu and Xinjiang, and reached the Mediterranean via Afghanistan, Iran, Iraq, Syria, and other countries, with Rome as the final destination. It became a route that connected ancient Eastern and Western civilizations. For thousands of years, people along the Silk Road traded in goods and had extensive religious, political, and cultural exchanges, generating a profound impact on the progress of Eastern and Western civilizations. There was also the "Maritime Silk Road" for trade by sea that started from coastal cities such as Guangzhou, Quanzhou, Hangzhou, and Yangzhou, passed through Southeast Asia and the Arabian Sea, and reached as far as the east coast of Africa.

Rather than merely a trade route, the ancient Silk Road fostered friendship. Friendly exchanges between China and other nations gave rise to the Silk Road Spirit, which promoted peace, cooperation, openness, inclusiveness, mutual learning, and mutual benefit. In 2013, China unveiled a major initiative

古代丝绸之路以全新的时代内涵，唤起了沿线国家的历史记忆，得到国际社会广泛支持。2014年，中国、哈萨克斯坦、吉尔吉斯斯坦联合申报的陆上丝绸之路东段“丝绸之路：长安—天山廊道的路网”入选世界文化遗产。古代丝绸之路为亚欧大陆商品物产大流通、科学技术大传播、思想观念大碰撞、多元文化大交融作出巨大贡献，也为当今世界和平与发展提供历史启迪。

calling for cooperation in building the "Belt & Road", reframing the ancient Silk Road in the context of a brand new era and giving it new meaning. The initiative brings back memories of fruitful exchanges between countries along the route, and has gained wide support from the international community. In 2014, the "Silk Roads: the Routes Network of Chang'an-Tianshan Corridor", the eastern section of the Silk Road, became a UNESCO World Heritage Site, after a joint application by China, Kazakhstan, and Kyrgyzstan was approved. The ancient Silk Road greatly contributed to the circulation of commodities, the dissemination of science and technology, the exchange of ideas, and the integration of diverse cultures on the Eurasian continent, providing inspiration for today's pursuit of world peace and development.

孔庙

孔庙是纪念中国古代思想家、教育家孔子的祠庙建筑，在古代承载着重要的政治、文化和教育意义。中国、朝鲜、日本、越南、印度尼西亚、新加坡、美国等国家建有2000多座孔庙。

曲阜孔庙位于孔子故里山东曲阜，始建于春秋时期（前478），以孔子故居为基础修建，是建造时间最早的一座孔庙。现存曲阜孔庙的主要建筑主要完成于明清两代，占地14万平方米，前后九进院落。庙内有殿堂、坛阁、门坊等460多间，沿南北向中轴线对称分布，四周围以红墙，整个庙宇气势恢宏、布局严谨，是中国现存规模最大的三大古建筑群之一。2000多年来，曲阜孔庙始终是儒家士大夫的精神圣殿，是中华文化的重要承载者。1994年，曲阜孔庙、孔林、孔府列入联合国教科文组织世界文化遗产名录。

Temples of Confucius

Temples of Confucius, built to commemorate the ancient Chinese philosopher and educator, had great political, cultural, and educational significance in ancient times. There are over 2,000 such temples located in countries such as China, South Korea, Japan, Vietnam, Indonesia, Singapore, and the United States.

The Temple of Confucius in Qufu, Shandong Province, where Confucius was born, has the longest history. It was first built in 478 B.C. during the Spring and Autumn period (770-476 B.C.) on the basis of Confucius' former residence. Its main existing structures were constructed in the Ming (1368-1644) and Qing (1616-1911) dynasties. Covering an area of 140,000 square meters, the temple complex consists of nine courtyards and over 460 buildings, including halls, pavilions, and gateway structures, all arranged symmetrically along the north-south axis. Surrounded by red walls, the temple radiates grandeur with an impressive layout. It is one of the largest and best-preserved ancient architectural complexes in China. For over 2,000 years, the temple has been seen as a spiritual sanctuary for Confucian scholars and remains an important symbol of Chinese culture. In 1994, the Temple, the Cemetery, and the Family Mansion of Confucius in Qufu were listed as a UNESCO World cultural Heritage Site.

长城

长城是中国古代的军事防御工程，是依托地形地势建造的高大、坚固且连绵不断的长垣与关隘，用以限隔敌方骑兵的行动。长城不单单是一道城墙，而是以城墙为主体，以隘口、军堡、关城、卫所、烽火台等多种防御工事连接形成的一套完整的防御体系，是中国古代一项伟大的建筑工程，也是人类文明史上的一大奇迹。

长城的修筑可追溯至西周时期。春秋战国时期，列国因战争防守需要而大量修筑长城。秦代统一中国后，将列国长城进行大规模修缮、连接，筑起了“万里长城”。此后直至明清时期，历朝历代几乎都有修筑长城的行动。长城的修筑延续2000多年，历代长城总计长度超过2.1万千米，各类遗存超过4.3万处。这样浩大的工程在中国和世界上都是绝无仅有的，人们因此将长城列为世界中古七大奇迹之一。目前，长城遗存主要分布在北方15个省区市，其代表性地段有山海关（河北）、嘉峪关（甘肃）、八达岭长城（北京）、

Great Wall

The Great Wall was ancient China's integrated defense system, consisting of a series of high and sturdy walls and passes built by exploiting natural geographical features to stop the assaults by enemy cavalry forces. Spanning its length are various fortifications, including passes, military fortresses, castles, garrison stations, and beacon towers, in addition to walls that served as the defense system's backbone. The Great Wall is an engineering marvel in ancient China and in the history of human civilization.

The history of the Great Wall can be traced back to the Western Zhou Dynasty (1046-771 B.C.). By the time of the Spring and Autumn period (770-476 B.C.), various states constructed extensive fortifications to protect their borders. When China was unified in the Qin Dynasty (221 B.C.-206 B.C.), sections of these earlier fortifications were repaired and linked to form the renowned "10,000-li Long Wall" (2 li approximately equal to 0.6 miles [1 kilometer]). From then on until the Ming (1368-1644) and Qing (1616-1911) dynasties, almost every dynasty took action to restore and rebuild the Great Wall. Over the course of more than 2,000 years, its length totaled more than 21,000 kilometers with over 43,000 historic sites. Such a colossal project is unparalleled in China and the world, earning it a spot among the "Seven Wonders of the Medieval World." Today, the remaining sections of the wall are primarily located in 15 provinces, autonomous regions, and municipalities in northern China; notable sections include the Shanhai-

司马台长城（北京）等。

长城具有丰富的地理、历史和文化内涵，其走向与中国北方的400毫米等降水量线基本吻合，是农耕文明和游牧文明的分界线，有效维护了二者之间的和平，为两种文明长时段、大规模、持续交流创造了稳定环境。长城的修建和戍守促进了中国古代汉族与少数民族的广泛融合，对中华民族多元一体格局的形成和发展作出重要贡献。以唐代的边塞诗为代表，古代的文人墨客以长城为题材创作了大量优秀的文艺作品，丰富了长城的文化内涵。长城凝结着中华民族几千年的智慧与力量，象征着中华民族大一统的政治传统和民族意志，近代以来更成为中华民族抗击侵略、维护统一的精神标识。1987年，长城列入联合国教科文组织世界文化遗产名录。

guan Pass in Hebei Province, the Jiayuguan Pass in Gansu Province, and the Badaling and Simatai sections in Beijing.

The Great Wall also has geographical, historical, and cultural significance. It stretches along the 400mm isoline of mean annual precipitation in northern China, serving as a dividing line between agricultural and nomadic civilizations and helping maintain peace between the agrarian and nomadic groups and facilitate long-term, large-scale, and continuous exchanges between them. The construction and defense of the Great Wall also promoted the extensive integration of the Han and ethnic minorities in ancient China, making significant contributions to the formation and development of a pluralistic and integrated Chinese nation. A large number of ancient literary masterpieces were based on the theme of the Great Wall, with the frontier poems of the Tang Dynasty (618-907) being the most prominent. These works add cultural meaning to the Great Wall. Over the centuries, the Great Wall has become a symbol of the Chinese nation's wisdom and strength, a testament to the Chinese people's political tradition of great unity. In modern times, it has also come to symbolize the Chinese nation's determination to resist aggression and protect unity. In 1987, it was included on the UNESCO World Cultural Heritage List.

秦始皇陵

秦始皇陵是中国古代史上第一位皇帝嬴政的陵园，位于陕西省西安市临潼区骊山脚下。秦始皇（前259—前210），原为战国时秦国国君，于前221年统一六国，建立起一个中央集权的统一的多民族国家。他建立了郡县制和官僚制，并统一了全国的文字、法律、度量衡、车轨，是中国历史上第一个使用“皇帝”称号的君主。

秦始皇陵建于前246年，是世界上规模最大、内涵最丰富的帝王陵墓之一。陵园仿秦朝都城咸阳城和宫城建造，整体呈南北长、东西窄的长方形，有内城和外城，坟丘坐落在内城南部。据史书记载，地宫内有各式宫殿、文武百官塑像、各种奇珍异宝，以及灌满水银的江河山川模型。秦始皇开创的陵园制度，对后代帝王产生了很大的影响。

陵园东北侧有兵马俑坑。坑道内兵马俑共同组成一个坐

Mausoleum of the First Qin Emperor

The Mausoleum of the First Qin Emperor, located at the foot of Lishan Mountain in Lintong District, Xi'an, Shaanxi Province, is the tomb of Ying Zheng (259-210 B.C.), China's first emperor. The First Qin Emperor, originally the ruler of the Qin State during the Warring States period (475-221 B.C.), unified the six states in 221 B.C. and founded a unified, centralized multiethnic country. He introduced county-based administrative divisions and a bureaucratic system, and standardized the Chinese writing system, laws, system of measurements, and carriage tracks. He was the first monarch in Chinese history to use the title of "emperor".

The mausoleum, built in 246 B.C., is one of the largest and most culturally significant imperial tombs in the world. It was designed to mirror Xianyang, the capital of the Qin Dynasty (221-206 B.C.), in terms of its urban layout and the way imperial palaces there were positioned. The mausoleum is rectangular, longer from north to south and narrower from east to west, consisting of an inner part and an outer part, with the burial mound located in the south within the inner wall. According to historical records, the mausoleum contains various palaces, with statues of civil and military officials, all kinds of treasures, and models of rivers and mountains filled with liquid mercury. The way that the First Qin Emperor built his mausoleum had a profound influence on how later emperors had their own tombs built.

The Terracotta Army is in the northeastern part of the mau-

西向东、排列有序、形态各异、气势磅礴的威严军阵，这些陶俑连同他们的战马、战车和武器，形象展示了秦始皇统率千军万马、威震四海的雄武神威，堪称泥塑艺术的杰作，具有极高的历史价值。1987年，秦始皇陵和兵马俑坑列入联合国教科文组织世界遗产名录。

soleum. East-facing terracotta warriors with different postures and facial expressions, along with terracotta horses, bronze chariots and weapons, stand in imposing battle array, representing the might and power of the emperor leading his troops to conquer his rivals and unify the country. The terracotta warriors are masterpieces of pottery art with unmatched historical value. In 1987, the Mausoleum of the First Qin Emperor and the Terracotta Army were designated a UNESCO World Heritage Site.

敦煌莫高窟

敦煌莫高窟是敦煌石窟群的代表窟群，位于甘肃省敦煌市东南的鸣沙山东麓断崖上，南北长1680米，高50米，700多个洞窟分布高低错落，是世界上现存规模最大、内容最丰富的佛教石窟群。

莫高窟始建于十六国的前秦时期（366），经历代开凿兴建，前后延续约1000年。莫高窟作为建筑、雕塑、壁画三者结合的立体艺术，其艺术形式既继承了本土汉晋艺术传统，吸收南北朝和唐宋美术风格，又不断接受、改造并融合域外印度、中亚和西亚的艺术风格，是中国石窟艺术发展演变的一个缩影。敦煌壁画技艺精湛，题材广泛，生动记录了古代社会生活的衣食住行、生老病死、婚丧嫁娶等民俗风情场景，以及古丝绸之路上的贸易往来和文化交流活动，为后世保留了珍贵的图像数据。近代以来，在莫高窟还发现了藏经洞，从中出土了4至11世纪的佛教经卷、社会文书、刺绣、绢画、法器等文物5万余件，被誉为“中国中古时代的

Mogao Caves

The Mogao Caves, the most prominent cave complex among the grottoes in Dunhuang, are located on the cliffs at the eastern foot of Mingsha Mountain in the southeast of Dunhuang, Gansu Province. It is 1,680 meters long from north to south, 50 meters high, and contains over 700 cells, making it the world's largest and most culturally significant Buddhist grottoes.

The Mogao Caves, first constructed in A.D. 366 during the Eastern Jin Dynasty (317-420), were expanded over the course of about 1,000 years. These caves represent an art form that combines architecture, sculpture, and mural painting, showcasing the evolvement of Chinese grotto art, which blends the artistic traditions of the Han and Jin dynasties with those of the Northern and Southern dynasties (420-589) and the Tang (618-907) and Song (907-1279) dynasties together with imported and transformed artistic styles from India, Central Asia, and West Asia. The Dunhuang murals, painted with exquisite techniques and covering a wide range of themes, vividly depict various aspects of the ancient Chinese society, such as clothing, food, housing, transportation, rituals of marriage and burial, and trade and cultural exchanges along the ancient Silk Road, preserving valuable information for later generations. In modern times, a library cave was discovered at the cave complex, which contains over 50,000 cultural artefacts such as Buddhist sutras, documents, works of embroidery, silk paintings, and ritual implements dating back to the 4th to 11th century. It

百科全书”。敦煌石窟和文献的丰富内涵与珍贵价值，受到世界各国学者的关注，并由此衍生出敦煌学研究。

敦煌莫高窟既是中国古代文明的艺术宝库，也是古代丝绸之路上不同文明之间交流互鉴的重要见证。莫高窟的千年发展过程与宗教、语言文字、文学艺术、历史地理、科技、经济、民族等有着直接的联系，连接起欧亚大陆的交流史、遍及亚洲的佛教传播史。1987年，敦煌莫高窟列入联合国教科文组织世界文化遗产名录。

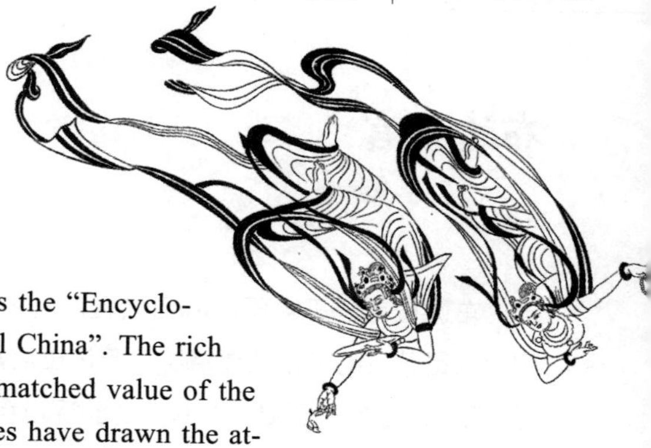

became known as the "Encyclopedia of Medieval China". The rich meanings and unmatched value of the Dunhuang grottoes have drawn the attention of scholars around the world, and Dunhuang has emerged as an academic focus area.

The Mogao Caves are not only a treasure trove of ancient Chinese civilization but also an important testament to the exchanges and mutual learning among civilizations along the ancient Silk Road. The evolvement of these caves over the thousand years was directly related to such factors as religious practices, language and writing, literature and art, history, geography, technology, economic development, and ethnicity. They record exchanges across the Eurasian continent and the spread of Buddhism throughout Asia. In 1987, the Mogao Caves were included on the UNESCO World Heritage List.

布达拉宫

布达拉宫位于中国西藏自治区首府拉萨市区西北的红山上，是著名的宫堡式建筑群。布达拉宫始建于公元6世纪松赞干布（617—650）时期，后于17世纪由五世达赖喇嘛（1617—1682）在其旧址上重修宫殿，称作“布达拉宫”，并作为历代达赖喇嘛的冬宫居所，成为旧时西藏农奴社会政教合一的统治中心。

布达拉宫占地40万平方米，建筑面积13万平方米，宫体主楼13层，高110多米。宫殿主体采用石木结构依山而建，具有鲜明的藏式风格，其花岗石墙体、白玛草墙领、金碧辉煌的金顶形成红、白、黄三种色彩的鲜明对比，并与独特建筑型体相互辉映，体现了以藏族为主，汉、蒙、满等各族能工巧匠高超的技艺水平，被誉为“高原圣殿”。

Potala Palace

The Potala Palace is a famous palace-style architectural complex located on the Red Hill in the northwest of Lhasa, the capital city of China's Xizang (Tibet) Autonomous Region. It was first built during the reign of Songtsen Gambo (617-650) and was later rebuilt under the direction of the 5th Dalai Lama (1617-1682) on the original site and named the "Potala Palace". It served as the winter residence for successive Dalai Lamas, and became the political and religious center of Tibet's old serf society.

The Potala Palace covers an area of 400,000 square meters, with a floor area of 130,000 square meters. Its main building has 13 floors and is over 110 meters high. The palace, with a distinctive Tibetan style, was built with stone and wood on a hill. Its white granite walls and red walls and golden roofs stand in sharp contrast with each other, complementing its unique architectural style. The palace, known as the "Holy Temple on the Plateau", showcases the superb craftsmanship of the Tibetan people, as well as that of the Han, Mongolian, Manchu and other ethnic groups.

布达拉宫收藏和保存了丰富的文物、典籍、珍品，堪称一座建筑艺术与佛教艺术的博物馆，也是中华民族团结和国家统一的重要实证，对于研究中国西藏政治、经济、历史、文化等都具有重要价值。1994年，布达拉宫列入联合国教科文组织世界文化遗产名录。

With a rich collection of cultural artefacts, classics, and treasures, the Potala Palace is a museum of architectural art and Buddhist art. An important testament to China's ethnic and national unity, it is also valuable to the research into Tibet's politics, economy, history, and culture. In 1994, the Potala Palace was designated a UNESCO World Heritage Site.

北京故宫

北京故宫是明清两代的皇家宫殿，原称“紫禁城”，位于北京中轴线的中心，占地面积约72万平方米，建筑面积约15万平方米，有大小院落70多座，房屋约9000余间，是世界上现存规模最大、保存最完整的木结构宫殿建筑群之一。

故宫内建筑分为外朝和内廷两部分，外朝的中心为太和殿、中和殿、保和殿，是明清朝廷举行大典礼的地方；内廷的中心是乾清宫、交泰殿、坤宁宫，是明清皇帝和皇后居住的正宫。故宫四面围有高10米的城墙，四角配以角楼，城外有宽52米的护城河。故宫黄瓦红墙，庄严宏伟，在细节和整体上讲究对称平衡。

今天的故宫不仅是中国古代建筑技艺的杰出代表，也是

Palace Museum

The Palace Museum, once known as the Forbidden City, was the imperial palace of the Ming (1368-1644) and Qing (1616-1911) dynasties. Situated at the center of the Central Axis of Beijing, it covers roughly 720,000 square meters with a build-up area of around 150,000 square meters. This magnificent complex boasts over 70 courtyards of varying sizes and more than 9,000 rooms, making it one of the world's largest and most impeccably preserved wooden-structured palace complex.

The Palace Museum consists of two main parts: the outer court and the inner court. The outer court includes the Hall of Supreme Harmony (*taihe dian*), Hall of Central Harmony (*zhonghe dian*), and Hall of Preserving Harmony (*baohe dian*). They were the venues for the emperor's court and grand audiences. The inner court centers around three halls, namely, the Palace of Heavenly Purity (*qianqing gong*), Hall of Union (*jiaotai dian*), and Palace of Earthly Tranquility (*kunning gong*). They were used as the emperor and empress's private quarters during the Ming and Qing dynasties. The Palace Museum is surrounded by 10-metre-high walls and a 52-metre-wide moat, with turret towers on each of the four corners. The elaborate and symmetrical arrangement of the palace's details, coupled with the golden tiles adorning its rooftops and the rusty red clay of its walls, imbue the structure with an air of solemn majesty.

The Palace Museum is not only a masterpiece of ancient Chinese architecture, but also a globally acclaimed museum of

享誉世界的古代文化艺术博物馆。据统计，故宫博物院现有藏品达186万多件，涵盖绘画、书法、陶瓷、铜器、玉器、织绣、甲骨文、古建筑、图书典籍、历史档案等众多门类，兼具历史、艺术、建筑、宫廷文化等多重博物馆特色，是明清时期中华文明的集中展现，也是全人类的珍贵文化遗产。

故宫将“天人之际”“礼乐复合”的中华优秀思想文化发扬光大，既体现出强烈的民族融合色彩，亦有“西学东渐”以来中外文化交融的特质，是中华文明“有容乃大”智慧的生动例证，是中华民族当之无愧的“大成之城”。

ancient culture and art. It houses over 1.86 million artefacts, encompassing painting, calligraphy, ceramics, bronze, jade, embroidery, oracle bone scripts, ancient architecture, books and classics, historical archives, and more. A showcase of Chinese civilization during the Ming and Qing dynasties, the museum is an invaluable cultural treasure for all of humanity.

The Palace Museum represents an example illustrating China's cultural concepts of "great enlightenment derived from harmony between heaven and man" and "integration of rites and music". In addition to showcasing national cohesiveness, the museum also highlights what came out of the exchanges between Chinese and foreign cultures after Western learning was introduced to China. It demonstrates the inclusiveness of Chinese civilization, which has contributed to what the Chinese nation has achieved.

天坛

天坛始建于明代永乐十八年（1420），是明清两代皇帝祭祀上天、祈求五谷丰登的场所。天坛坐落在北京市南部，占地约273万平方米，坛域北呈圆形，南为方形，象征“天圆地方”。

天坛分内坛和外坛，主要建筑集中于内坛，内坛分为南北两个建筑群，这是中国现存最大的古代祭祀性建筑群，也是世界上最大的祭天建筑群。天坛北为祈谷坛，用于春季祈祷丰年，其中心建筑是祈年殿，三层重檐的圆形宝顶独具特色，殿内中央的四根立柱寓意一年四季，外围两排各有12根柱子分别代表十二月、十二时辰。南为圜丘坛，专门用于冬至日祭天。“圜丘”是一座巨大圆形石台，其台阶、石栏板数量均采用“九”和“九”的倍数，呼应九重天，强调天

Temple of Heaven

The Temple of Heaven, completed in 1420 during the 18th year of the reign of the Ming Emperor Yongle, was a site where the emperors of the Ming and Qing dynasties offered sacrifices to Heaven and prayed for bountiful harvests. Situated in the southern part of Beijing, the temple spans 2.73 square kilometers of parkland. The altar area is round in the north and square in the south, reflecting the belief that heaven is round and earth is square.

The Temple of Heaven is divided into the inner part and outer part, with the main buildings being in the inner area. The inner area is further divided into two architectural groups in the north and south. It is the largest existing imperial sacrificial building complex in China and the world's largest existing building complex for offering sacrifice to heaven. The Altar of Prayer for Good Harvests (*qigu tan*) is situated in the north and is used for praying for good harvests in spring. The Hall of Prayer for Good Harvests (*qinian dian*), located at the center, is a circular, three-tiered building with a conical roof. Its four inner, 12 middle and 12 outer pillars, represent the four seasons, 12 months and 12 traditional Chinese hours, respectively. The Circular Mound Altar (*yuanqiu tan*), situated in the south, was used exclusively for emperors to offer sacrifices to heaven on the day of the Winter Solstice. It is a round terrace on marble stones. The number of its steps and slates all circular around the number nine, symbolizes the "nine circles of heaven," emphasizing the supremacy of heaven. The two altars are con-

的至高无上。南、北两坛之间以甬道相连，共同形成贯通天坛建筑南北1200米的中轴线。

天坛建筑宏伟壮丽、庄严肃穆，集明清两代建筑技艺之大成，又以大面积树林植被营造良好的生态环境，从单一建筑到整体布局都展现着中国古人“天人合一”的宇宙观。1998年，天坛列入联合国教科文组织世界文化遗产名录。

nected by a walkway, forming the central axis of the Temple of Heaven, which spans 1,200 meters from north to south.

The Temple of Heaven boasts a grand and magnificent construction style that showcases the pinnacle of architectural techniques from the Ming and Qing dynasties. The trees and shrubs surrounding the area contribute to a pleasant ecological environment. This reflects the ancient Chinese concept of "harmony between humanity and nature", apparent in how individual structures were designed and positioned as well as the overall layout of the temple complex was planned. In 1998, the Temple of Heaven was included on the UNESCO World Cultural Heritage List.

中国古代朝代对照简表

时代 / 王朝	起止时间
五帝	约前30世纪初—约前21世纪初
夏	约前2070—约前1600年
商	前1600—前1046年
周	前1046—前256年
西周	前1046—前771年
东周	前770—前256年
春秋	前770—前 476年
战国	前475—前 221年
秦	前221—前 206年
汉	前206—220年
西汉	前206—25年
东汉	25—220年
三国	220—280年
魏	220—265年
蜀	221—263年
吴	222—280年
晋	265—420年
西晋	265—317年
东晋	317—420年

CHRONOLOGY OF ANCIENT CHINESE HISTORY

PERIOD / DYNASTY	TIME SPAN
Period of the Five Legendary Rulers	c. early 30th century B.C.- c. early 21st century B.C.
Xia Dynasty	c. 2070-1600 B.C.
Shang Dynasty	1600-1046 B.C.
Zhou Dynasty	1046-256 B.C.
Western Zhou Dynasty	1046-771 B.C.
Eastern Zhou Dynasty	770-256 B.C.
Spring and Autumn Period	770-476 B.C.
Warring States Period	475-221 B.C.
Qin Dynasty	221-206 B.C.
Han Dynasty	206 B.C.-A.D. 220
Western Han Dynasty	206B.C.-A.D. 25
Eastern Han Dynasty	A.D. 25-220
Three Kingdoms	220-280
Kingdom of Wei	220-265
Kingdom of Shu	221-263
Kingdom of Wu	222-280
Jin Dynasty	265-420
Western Jin Dynasty	265-317
Eastern Jin Dynasty	317-420

时代 / 王朝	起止时间
南北朝	420—589年
南朝	420—589年
北朝	386—581年
隋	581—618年
唐	618—907年
五代十国	907—960年
宋	960—1279年
北宋	960—1127年
南宋	1127—1279年
辽	907—1125年
西夏	1038—1227年
金	1115—1234年
元	1206—1368年
明	1368—1644年
清	1616—1911年

PERIOD / DYNASTY	TIME SPAN
Northern and Southern Dynasties	420-589
Southern Dynasties	420-589
Northern Dynasties	386-581
Sui Dynasty	581-618
Tang Dynasty	618-907
Five Dynasties and Ten Kingdoms	907-960
Song Dynasty	960-1279
Northern Song Dynasty	960-1127
Southern Song Dynasty	1127-1279
Liao Dynasty	907-1125
Xixia Dynasty	1038-1227
Jin Dynasty	1115-1234
Yuan Dynasty	1206-1368
Ming Dynasty	1368-1644
Qing Dynasty	1616-1911

词条音序排列表

ENTRIES IN ALPHABETICAL ORDER

图书在版编目（CIP）数据

中国关键词. 传统文化标识篇：汉英对照 / 中国外文出版发行事业局, 当代中国与世界研究院, 中国翻译研究院著；李慧如等译. -- 北京：朝华出版社, 2023.8
ISBN 978-7-5054-5223-7
Ⅰ. ①中… Ⅱ. ①中… ②当… ③中… ④李… Ⅲ. ①中国特色社会主义—社会主义建设模式—研究—汉、英 ②中华文化—研究—汉、英 Ⅳ. ①D616②K203
中国国家版本馆CIP数据核字(2023)第060972号

中国关键词：传统文化标识篇（汉英对照）

作　　者　中国外文出版发行事业局　当代中国与世界研究院
中国翻译研究院
英文翻译　李慧如　许汝艺　郭翊明　于　泓
英文改稿　David Ferguson [英]
英文审定　朱　渊　蔡力坚
特约编辑/项目统筹　申　阳
项目执行　华光灿
翻译统筹　赵维真　吴晓蕊
责任编辑　赵　倩　张北鱼
责任印制　陆竞赢　崔　航
装帧设计　杜　帅
出版发行　朝华出版社
社　　址　北京西城区百万庄大街24号　**邮政编码**　100037
出版合作　（010）68995532
订购电话　（010）68996522
传　　真　（010）88415258（发行部）
联系版权　zhbq@cicg.org.cn
网　　址　http: //zhcb.cicg.org.cn
印　　刷　天津中印联印务有限公司
经　　销　全国新华书店
开　　本　880mm × 1230mm　1 / 32　　**字　　数**　115千字
印　　张　13.125
版　　次　2023年8月第1版　2023年8月第1次印刷
装　　别　平
书　　号　ISBN 978-7-5054-5223-7
定　　价　78.00元
